The HOME Remodeler

Plans & Ideas for 31 Outstanding Remodeling Projects

Stouffer & Smith Architects

Written by
Christina B. Farnsworth

HOME PLANNERS, INC.
TUCSON, ARIZONA

Photo: Richard Gross

Adding an island improves the work triangle in the kitchen (above). The island houses the cook top.

Kitchen Project (cover) and Bath Project (page 8, bottom) both designed by **Sergio Zeballos, Architect,** Los Angeles, California

Photographs
Brewster & Brewster Photography:
  Front Cover, 5, 8
Samuel Fein, used courtesy of
  Professional Builder & Remodeler:
  Back Cover
Ewing Galloway: 16
Bob Greenspan/Midwestock:
  Title Page, 10, 14
Richard Gross: Table of Contents, 3, 8
Kent Oppenheimer: 4, 5, 6, 9, 11, 12, 13
Gary I. Rothstein/Redstone Agency: 7
Gunther Schabestiel: 15

Published by Home Planners, Inc.
Editorial and Corporate Office:
  3275 West Ina Road, Suite 110
  Tucson, Arizona 85741
Distribution Center:
  29333 Lorie Lane
  Wixom, Michigan 48393
Chairman: Charles W. Talcott
President and Publisher:
  Rickard D. Bailey
Publications Manager:
  Cindy J. Coatsworth
Architectural Editor:
  John C. Shaheen, AIA
Editor: Christina B. Farnsworth
Book Design: Paul Fitzgerald

Library of Congress Catalogue
  Card Number: 92-74617
ISBN softcover: 0-918894-98-0
ISBN hardcover: 0-918894-99-9

First printing January 1993
10 9 8 7 6 5 4 3 2 1

CONTENTS

Front Cover: This dream kitchen meets the heart's desire of the most creative gourmet cook. Before remodeling it was a small, dark space in an otherwise up-to-date house. For more detailed information about this plan, see pages 38-39.

Back Cover: The luxury bathroom addition, shown here, equals its adjoining bedroom. Built as a tropical refuge from cold winters, it features a steam shower, spa, mini-kitchen and generous storage space. The kitchen is as practical as it is glamorous. The pine cabinets are English; counters are an unusual color of granite called uba-tuba; floors are St. Albain French limestone.

THE ART OF REMODELING

Photo: Richard Gross

Photo: Richard Gross

A skylight-and-window bay pops
out beyond the eaves to capture
needed light (above). It also improves
circulation through the room and
allows for comfortable furniture
arrangement.

Even small kitchen remodelings
can include heavy-duty storage
space (above). Pull-out drawers
maximize pantry storage.

Photo: Richard Gross

Careful design gives this master
bedroom remodel a luxury bathroom plus needed closet space
(right). Elevated wood stove nestled
in tile nook adds warmth and eye
appeal.

KITCHEN REMODELING

Greenhouse addition (right) brightens both breakfast nook and kitchen. Center island is a serious workspace with both cooktop and sink.

The view from this breakfast nook (below) shows two work triangles. The cooking and clean-up work triangle includes double sink and dishwasher along the wall and the island cooktop. Refrigerator and island vegetable sink form second workspace.

"Before" pictures show just how dull a big kitchen can look (above right and right). Big kitchens often have work triangles that are too spread out. Added island and greenhouse (above) brighten the room and improve function.

Windows beneath upper cabinets plus a large skylight illuminate this luxurious kitchen remodel (top left). Granite counters and back-splashes, parquet floors, commercial cooktop and custom range hood are among special features.

The shape is the same, but it takes some looking to recognize the old kitchen (left) in the new (above). Reorganizing appliances, adding windows and upgrading materials created a radical facelift without major construction.

This "before" kitchen feels cramped and cluttered (above). Remodeled kitchen wastes no space (left). Tall upper cabinets reach to the ceiling. For convenience, the microwave is built in next to the refrigerator.

What a difference a bay makes. "Before" kitchen was narrow, compartmentalized galley with no breakfast area (above). New, bowed bay with French doors and sidelights adds European appeal and lights the breakfast area (right). Double-door pantry storage, decorative tile backsplash and glass doors are custom touches.

Stove area shows similar improvements from old to new (above and right). Lengthening kitchen allowed moving refrigerator to opposite wall and adding built-in ovens. New cooktop has 18-inch workspaces on either side.

This kitchen with its many doorways is a major circulation problem. Before (left), it was chock-a-block with awkward cabinets and too-dark counters.

After remodeling, this simple design (left) takes on new spirit with angled base cabinets and counters. Wood cabinets anchor the kitchen; light-colored counters make it feel larger. Angled counters ease traffic flow through kitchen.

Compare the old (left) and the new (above). Old kitchen's dark counters and white cabinets are discordant. New kitchen offers plenty of counter space on either side of the refrigerator. Counter nearest dining room serves as staging area for formal meals.

BATHROOM REMODELING

Master bathroom addition (right) has every feature and all the storage anyone could want — plus stained-glass doors leading to a secret garden.

Before (above) this bathroom was okay but not great. It had easy-to-clean tile surfaces. New bathroom sizzles with style (right). Ceiling now follows the roof slope, and pop-out makes space for larger tub and a tile shelf/ seat. Glass block brings in light without sacrificing privacy. Design would also work for dormer or attic renovation.

Dressing area (above) didn't work very hard before remodeling. Incorporating it into the master bathroom allows compartmentalization of bathing and grooming spaces (left). Notice clerestory window above vanity mirror.

Even the toilet paper is about to run out on this tired old bath (above). Re-arranging fixtures improves both function and style (left). Tucking toilet into nook beside vanity takes it off center stage. Large mirror above vanity makes the room read wider.

LIVING ROOM REMODELING

Greenhouse-like addition brings outdoors in and adds another floor of living space. Compare with the before (below left) and the exterior on page 14. Now those big windows really deliver the picture!

Photo: Bob Greenspan/MIDWESTOCK © 1989

The interior (above) before remodeling feels enclosed and dark despite great water views. Grand piano dominates the room.

Photo: Bob Greenspan/MIDWESTOCK © 1989

View from new stairway highlights commercial-grade railings and inventive balustrades. Plan is open without sacrificing safety or views. Added gallery/loft crowns kitchen and dining rooms. Note visible hint of family room beyond two-sided fireplace.

Only picture and hearth remain the same after family-room remodel (left). Flat ceilings replace awkward beams (below). Stripping curtains and adding built-ins completely recasts the room. Living room (below) is from same house.

Photo: Kent Oppenheimer

Low, heavily beamed ceilings and large fireplace dominate this room (above) before remodel.

Photo: Kent Oppenheimer

Before remodel (below), this room has no focal point. Furniture placement is unappealing. Heavy, irregular beams make room awkward despite cathedral ceiling.

Often, even a simple facelift makes a world of difference. Full wall of glass is main focal point in this large living room (above) after remodel. Crown moldings add sophistication and furniture grouping provides multiple conversation groups. Kitchen (page 4) and dining room (page 13) are results of the same remodel.

Photo: Kent Oppenheimer

Photo: Kent Oppenheimer

Photo: Kent Oppenheimer

After remodeling, shutters modulate light from living-room pop-out (above). Adding just a few feet gives the room a focal point and space for several conversation areas. Before remodel (left), built-ins at one end of the room gave it informal familial feeling Dining room, page 13, bottom, is from same house.

DINING ROOM REMODELING

Just as in the living room (page 11), "before" dining room lacks focal point (left). It's big but boring. Attentive details add glamour (below). French doors, wainscotting, hardwood floors and crown molding add warmth and sophistication.

Small details, properly used, make dramatic changes. Plain-Jane dining room (above) gets new lease on life by replacing aluminum sliders with wood-framed, divided-lite French doors (left). Crown moldings and wainscotting dress up room for company. Dining room is from same house as living room on page 12.

The Art of Remodeling **13**

EXTERIOR REMODELING

This contemporary home (right) was functional before, but too small with dated exterior. Entry was lost under the deck. Deep eaves shaded windows; inside was dark. Before and after interiors are on page 10.

Greenhouse-like addition floods the interior with light (above). Two-story entry projects beyond original deck, bringing attention to front door. Horizontal bands emphasize updated deck, minimize garage. For safety, remodel includes taller chimney.

Many older single-story homes provide adequate shelter, but not much pizzazz (left). Mandatory side yards and set-backs can severely limit space for horizontal growth.

Second-floor addition and full facelift (left) dramatically change character and double floor space of single-story home. Note how new shed roof highlights and shields entry. Varied roof lines and projecting bay add curb appeal to facade.

With any work in progress (left), there is considerable demolition and mess before second-floor addition and new entry can take shape. However, owners still have safe haven inside from remodeling storm.

REMODELING BASICS

WHY REMODEL?

Every time you round a certain corner in your kitchen, you bump your hip.

You're tired of climbing over the side of your bathtub and slip-sliding into the shower.

You find you need numbered tickets like the deli uses to thread the family through the morning wake-up process and get everyone out the door in time. "Hey, hurry-up in there," seems to be the slogan for your mornings.

The kids are getting older, the noise level in your home is simply unbearable, and there is nowhere to hide.

You've really gotten into exercise, but your favorite machines take up most of your bedroom, or you have to exercise in the dark, cold basement.

You need more... (fill in the blank).

At one time or another, for any of the reasons above, the house that fit you just fine when you bought it, doesn't fit right any more.

DECIDING TO REMODEL

Lack of space is one of the primary reasons to remodel. Many older homes simply weren't designed with family rooms — such homes predate big-screen television, sur-round-sound stereo and Nintendo.

Often older homes have purely utilitarian master bathrooms or none at all. In dual-income families, the husband and wife often must wake up, clean up and get out of the house at the same time every day. A single lavatory sink in the master bathroom just doesn't serve family needs.

Older kitchens are often too small with cramped working areas and no informal dining space. Many have no room for a dishwasher, a microwave or the other appliances that have become kitchen essentials. The existing cabinets, counter surfaces and appliances may be wornout or outdated.

Our hobbies now take up more space than they once did, too. Many families are trying to find space for home exercise equipment, media rooms or teen retreats.

Whatever the reason, remodeling your home can be the right solution, but how do you decide whether to remodel or move?

The first thing to do is walk around your neighborhood. Is your current neighborhood an important part of your lifestyle? Is your house already the biggest and most expensive on the block? Are other people remodeling their homes? Do you like the school? Are the travel-times to your church, your favorite grocery store, and other frequent destinations reasonable to you?

Will you continue to like your neighborhood? Is it changing? Is industry moving in? Are you in an airport runway path? Will traffic increase? Will shopping areas continue to be readily available?

In deciding whether to remodel, ask yourself if you want to stay in your neighborhood. Define what you like about where you live now. Walk around your neighborhood. If you live in the smallest house on a block of large homes, you can be a sure-fire winner with a tasteful remodel.

You need to weigh what you can afford against what you need. Remodeling costs will surprise you. Sometimes spending more for remodeling results in more comfort and less maintenance throughout the life of the home. Only you can decide.

If your house is the biggest and most expensive on the block, you should pause and think seriously about remodeling it. Owners seldom recover the cost in making the best even better. You may want to think about moving, but maybe you love that old maple tree in the backyard too much to consider a new house — that's OK, too.

If you have roots in your neighborhood, like it and the local amenities, you should probably upgrade your home. Your bottom line in deciding whether or not to remodel is "can I afford to remodel and will it enhance my life and give me pleasure?" To answer "yes" is often enough.

Moreover, there are substantial costs to moving. Should you decide to move rather than remodel, you'll have to spend money to spruce up your house to be competitive in today's tight real estate market. Costs of moving include realtor commissions, transfer taxes and lawyer fees — these are often in the range of 10 percent of the selling price of your home. You will have to keep your house model-home clean all the time so that the realtor can show it to prospective buyers. You will also have to pack or pay someone else to pack up your belongings, and then spend more money to move them to your new home.

There will be fees and taxes to

pay on the new-home acquisition as well. Plus, you'll have to unpack. You'll want to paint and redecorate the new home, too. Some of your furniture won't fit. Well, you get the drift. Remodeler Mark vanReuth of Brighton Builders in Arnold, Maryland, told *Professional Builder & Remodeler*, the business magazine for the housing industry, that selling and moving costs typically add up to $25,000.

You will probably be surprised by the cost of remodeling, too. Builders who specialize in remodeling and local appraisers and realtors can offer you a ball-park estimate of the costs for a typical kitchen remodel, master-bedroom addition, family-room addition, exterior facelift or whatever improvement you want to make.

Remodeling consultant and magazine columnist, Steve Martindale points out that remodeling costs vary throughout the country. Even in major metropolitan areas costs vary widely. In Dallas, for example, it can cost as much as $100 a square foot for a room addition. In Washington, D.C., the same remodel could cost $120 a square foot. In San Francisco, one of the most expensive housing markets, it would cost as much as $150 a square foot, Martindale says.

Kitchens and bathrooms are what Martindale calls "product inten-

sive." The brand you select for your refrigerator, stove or dishwasher can make a big difference in your kitchen remodeling costs. Because bathrooms are small and pack many plumbing fixtures, electrical devices and storage units in a small number of square feet, they are the most expensive rooms to remodel on a per-square-foot basis.

Ball-park estimates only give you a very rough idea. Each remodeling project is different depending on the part of the country, the type of house, the type and scope of the remodeling project, variations in local building codes, the finish materials you choose and even the lay of the land your home is on.

The materials you select can radically alter the cost of your project. Owners of one luxury bathroom featured in a decorator magazine chose marble and marble tile for vanity counters, flooring and tub and shower surrounds. The cost? Nearly $7000 in a 200-square-foot master-bathroom remodel ($35 a square foot for the material alone). Choosing ceramic tile to finish the same surfaces would have cost about $5000, or $10 a square foot less.

Similarly, in an otherwise modest kitchen remodel, top-of-the-line built-in appliances cost more than $12,000 for a built-in refrigerator, cook-top, range-hood, ovens, microwave and super-quiet dishwasher.

The best houses look like they have evolved over time. A variety of details such as shutters can unify different shapes within an existing house and its additions. The best remodels maintain the original character or establish a unified new character for your home.

Be creative. A garage is a garage, but a studio apartment over a garage (plan R-128 on page 76) can provide much needed space. The apartment can be a get-away for parents, guest quarters or even provide rental income.

Choosing economical appliances of reasonable quality could cost less than $4000.

You will have to decide if you want the top of the line or the bottom in terms of products. A higher expenditure in the beginning can often result in lower maintenance costs. In an open-plan family room, the dishwasher is often so noisy that the family can't watch television while it is running. In such a situation, the extra cost of a quiet dishwasher may be justified.

Remember that remodeling does cost more than new construction. In remodeling, you have to tear out and throw away what you don't like before you can add the improvements you do want.

You or your contractor will have to arrange to have a dumpster delivered and taken away. If you have lead or asbestos in the house, it will have to be disposed of according to new environmental rules. It will cost a surprising amount to get rid of what you no longer want.

There are general common sense rules about remodeling. If all of the homes in your neighborhood have three bedrooms and two bathrooms, you can safely add a bedroom and bathroom to your two-bedroom, one-bathroom home. If, however, you are adding on so much that your home doesn't fit the neighborhood, it may actually become harder to sell in the future.

Experts agree that remodeling should complement the existing house and give it strong curb appeal. You should not overbuild for your neighborhood. You should use energy-saving items such as low-flow shower heads, "programmable" thermostats, and low-E or double-glazed windows. Remodeling work should be done in a professional manner.

You should also respect your mature landscape. Some experts say that each full-grown tree on a property can add as much as $1000 to its value. Some of the most beautiful remodels wrap around desirable landscape specimens. You will also need to protect trees and other valuable vegetation. Heavy equipment can compress soil and roots and kill beautiful trees.

Will you get back the money you spend on remodeling when you sell your home? Probably not all of it, though it depends on what you remodel and where you live. If you live in a laminate-counter neighborhood, you can pretty much kiss the extra cost of marble or granite counters good-bye. On the other hand, if you really like the low maintenance and high durability of granite, why not have it?

Many magazines have attempted pay-back studies. Some interview realtors and others interview appraisers or remodelers. These professionals can give good ball-park estimates for their regions. However, these surveys are matters of opinion from selected professionals in each surveyed market — such

studies are anecdotal rather than scientifically valid.

Practical Homeowner magazine surveys appraisers to produce annual payback studies. They quote Oregon appraiser Chuck Fisher, who says, "Cosmetics sell homes." High on *Practical Homeowner's* list of improvements that pay is an exterior facelift.

Kitchens, bathrooms, additions over the garage and attic conversions ranked well in their list of top-10 remodeling projects. Estimated paybacks for specific improvements ranged from 48 to 91 percent.

Professional Builder & Remodeler, the business magazine for the housing industry, tried to get a handle on pay-back costs, too. The magazine discovered that Chicago-based Airoom, designers and builders of between 50 and 150 room additions a year, keeps some of the best data on pay back. Airoom's subsidiary, Lamb Financial Services, offers financing for remodeling jobs. Thus Airoom has been able to compile comparisons based on the appraised value of the home before remodeling and its value right after completion of the project.

As an example, Airoom added a room addition costing $41,000 to a house that had an "as-is" appraisal of $105,000 in Libertyville, a distant Chicago suburb. After the remodel, appraisers figured the house value at $136,000. The $41,000 cost had a project value of $31,000, therefore, 75.6% of the remodeling cost would be recouped if the house sold right after the remodel. In another example, a $28,800 remodel of an as-is appraised $110,000 house would recoup 62.5% of its remodeling cost.

Pay back can be much more, if you are remodeling a house in a prestigious area. Airoom added a $45,900 room addition to a house in Glencoe, Ill. Glencoe is one of Chicago's prestige suburbs along the North Shore of Lake Michigan. The as-is appraisal was $265,000. After completion of the remodeling, appraisers pegged house value at $320,000. In this case, the $45,900 remodeling had a value of $55,000. Cost recouped? An astounding 119.8 percent of the cost of the improvement!

Many homeowners who like to remodel look to buy the oldest house or the smallest house on a block of large houses. In terms of pay back it is best not to be the pioneer — the first to remodel — but to be one of the last to bring a substandard house up to neighborhood standards.

Anticipating pay-back value may not be the best way to decide whether or not to remodel. When you sell your house, buyers will expect a sound roof, a good furnace and so forth. If you need to replace your roof or your furnace or air-conditioning, you would simply do it without worrying about whether or not you would recoup the cost at resale. Your decision process would revolve around quality and value — what is the best product at the best cost that will do the job and keep you safe and comfortable?

In real estate markets where there are more houses than buyers, outdated houses simply won't sell. If buyers can get houses with up-to-date kitchens, master suites and room additions, why buy houses that don't have desired features?

In survey after survey, kitchens and bathrooms are the most popular rooms to remodel. Family rooms and master bedroom suites are the most popular to add. Surveys published by realtors and business and popular magazines find over and over again that up-to-date kitchens and bathrooms sell both new and existing homes.

Knowing what buyers of new

A facelift can dramatically alter a home's appearance. Plan R-122 (shown in detail on page 82) illustrates how changing windows, and adding gables and a wrap-around porch make a typical two-story house seem larger and give it more curb appeal.

Small additions can result in big changes. The kitchen portion of plan R-102 (shown also on page 32) is roughly 11-feet-square. High ceilings expand space visually. Practical design provides more than 20 feet of counter space and a great work triangle.

homes want can also help you decide how and what to remodel. If you choose to sell your home, you will be competing with new homes for sale as well as other existing homes. *Professional Builder & Remodeler* annually surveys both new home buyers and those planning to remodel to find out what they want. In their 19th annual new home survey, the magazine found that the average buyer continues to prefer a traditional-style house with three bedrooms and two bathrooms.

Approximately 30 percent of surveyed buyers wanted four bedrooms and 2½-bathrooms. Sixty percent or more wanted first-floor master suites, rooms with cathedral ceilings, covered entries, porches and patios. Half of all surveyed buyers wanted a room they could use for a den, library or office. They wanted their master suites to have walk-in closets, private bathrooms and separation from the other bedrooms.

When asked what made the best and deepest impression as they shopped, consumers answered open floor plan, kitchen, master bedroom, living room and family room in that order.

Professional Builder & Remodeler also surveys consumers planning to remodel their homes. Kitchens, bathrooms and room additions are the three most-popular remodeling projects.

Changes these consumers planned to make in their kitchens included changing the floor plan, increasing cabinet space, upgrading cabinets, and adding a pantry, lighting, new appliances and windows. Nearly half of the survey respondents wanted to create enough space for an eating area in their kitchen. Perhaps their desires reflect the trend for more informal living.

Changing and upgrading fixtures were top priorities for remodeling a bathroom as well. Walk-in closets, added windows, skylights and separate showers were among the most desired changes.

Among surveyed remodeling consumers, the purposes of planned room additions ran the gamut from adding a formal dining space to adding bathrooms. Nearly as many people chose "other" as chose a specific purpose for their room addition. Space for family entertainment and an area for a full- or part-time office scored well. Survey results seemed to show that there are as many reasons for adding a room as there are consumers.

When all is said and done, the final decision is yours. You should make your home live well for you.

CAN YOU DO WHAT YOU WANT?

Most communities have requirements for set-backs and side yards and how much of your lot the house can cover. Some communities restrict height. Others, primarily in scenic areas, may limit houses to shapes or heights that don't obstruct light or views for other homeowners.

Some master-planned communities and historic neighborhoods have restrictions on style and color.

Your local building officials can tell you what the zoning requirements are in your area. Master-planned communities and historic neighborhoods will have architectural guidelines.

If what you plan to do differs from zoning regulations, you can apply for a building code variance. Typically, these require that you have a set of plans for the remodeling project. In some communities you need to have written permission from neighbors that surround your property. In other communities, you need to "go before the zoning board" to present your case. Once again, your local governing agencies can tell you how to proceed.

You'll need to check with a local builder or architect to see if what you want to do is economically feasible. Almost anything can be built, but if plumbing runs are too long to make good sewer connections, if there are peculiarities in soil conditions or in the way a site slopes, the cost of a remodeling project can rapidly become prohibitively expensive. Often a professional can suggest an alternative approach that will still accomplish what you want within a reasonable budget.

A designer can also help you make sure that the design you like will actually solve living problems. A designer, architect or builder/remodeler can tell you if the addition overwhelms the house, whether or not it will improve circulation space and traffic flow through the

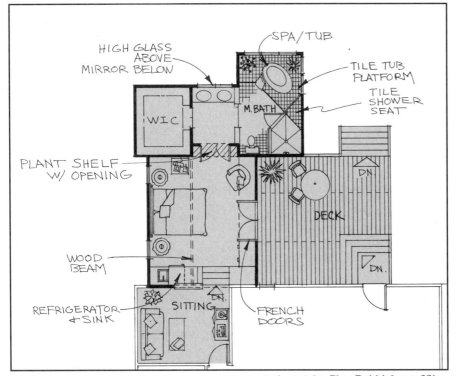

Adding a master suite can make a cramped house fit just right. Plan R-111 (page 62) converts an existing bedroom into a sitting room that leads to the master-suite wing. The wing has a mini-kitchen, a spacious bedroom, plenty of closet space and a luxurious master bathroom.

house and how it will relate to other areas within the existing house.

HOW TO PAY FOR
YOUR REMODEL

You should talk to local lenders and do some math to figure out the best method to pay for your remodeling project. When *Professional Builder & Remodeler*, with the help of National Family Opinion Research, surveyed remodeling consumers, they found that home equity loans, home improvement loans, credit unions, personal loans, second mortgages, refinancing the existing house, loans against pension funds or 401K programs, construction loans and FHA loans are all sources of remodeling financing.

Home equity loans and loans against pension funds and 401K programs require the least amount of work on your part. Usually these loans are based on the value of the existing house or the amount of money you have in the program.

For other loans, you will need documentation: a full set of plans for the remodeling project, a budget, and a projected time estimate in which to complete the job. You will more than likely also need the kind of information you provided the lender for your mortgage: information on your income and your debts, an appraisal of your home to determine value, and possibly a survey. Lenders like to know what you are doing, how much it will cost, how long it will take and if you can pay for it.

Lenders also like you to have permits in hand — especially if the remodeling project involves getting a zoning variance.

SO YOU'VE DECIDED TO
REMODEL — NOW WHAT?

Talk to your friends, but don't let them scare you. Your friends will have heard of good remodelers — but they will also have horror stories about mega-budgets and projects gone awry.

Ask local building officials for suggestions of reputable remodelers. They inspect projects and will know who does a good job. If they are reluctant, ask them who they would use to remodel their own home.

You can save yourself heartache by thorough preparation.

First prepare a realistic budget. Talk to your lender. Talk to several builder/remodelers about ball-park estimates and believe them. Because you have to tear parts of the house apart before adding on, remodeling costs more than new construction.

There are often surprises. Maybe the plumbing runs aren't where

Whether you a hire a pro or do it yourself, you'll need to burn a little midnight oil. Do your homework to successfully plan your project. You'll need a budget, plans, and time estimates. Lenders will want to know what you are doing, how much it will cost, how long it will take and if you can pay for it—and so will you.

everyone thought they were. Perhaps when you tear out existing walls you find deterioration from moisture or damage from termites that has to be repaired. Maybe there is a site problem with inadequate drainage or rocks or unstable soils. All of these problems can be dealt with at a cost, but the cost may simply be too high.

Remember that you are going to chew up some of your existing landscaping. Budget for returning things to normal or better after the remodeling is over. Also plan to pay to preserve your mature landscaping. You may have to fence around trees to keep construction equipment from compacting soils and killing roots. Your foundation may have to be

hand dug if there is no other way to preserve mature specimens. Experts say that each mature tree can add as much as $1000 to the value of your home — it is worth a little extra to save valuable landscaping.

Allow 10 or 20 percent to your budget for surprises and extras. As you get into choosing materials, you may change your mind. You will feel inexplicably cheated if you can't

afford something you really like, and you'll think about it every day you continue to live in your home.

Be fair but firm with everyone you deal with. Remodeling is a business; remodelers are entitled to a profit. Wars and war stories come about because people feel they were cheated or treated unfairly. If you create an adversarial atmosphere by demanding the premium work for the cheapest price, you may be setting yourself up for a war. Price is not the only factor in choosing a remodeler.

If you think you can do the project yourself, think again. Unless you are extremely well-organized and a true craftsperson, you could end up with the "forever" remodeling project that actually damages the resale value of your home.

In *Practical Homeowner's* survey, the appraisers found under-improvement in about 13 percent of the houses they surveyed. Mary Ann Englert, a Bradenton, Fla., appraiser, told the magazine that under-improvement was usually the result of poor materials, workmanship or design.

You can use the best plan, but if you cut corners on materials or if craftsmanship is lacking, you can actually damage the value of your home.

Homeowner that professional work adds more value. Using a professional increased the value of the remodeled home from 24 to 39 percent compared to do-it-yourself remodels, according to the appraisers.

You can cut costs by taking on some clean-up or painting or some other task you feel comfortable with. However, spell out what you will do and be committed to doing it. If your work slows up the professionals, your project will take longer to complete and could end up costing you more money.

plumbing for a future bathroom or leave space for built-ins and complete those elements in a later remodel when your budget permits. You will still have a professional job that adds value to your home and your lifestyle, yet you will also be prepared for later additions that won't require undoing what you've just paid to have done.

Look at appliances, big-screen televisions, stereo equipment, sound systems, whirlpools, spas and all of the other home toys. Include the items and brands that you like depending on your budget. Just as you can stub-in plumbing for a future bathroom, you can also size your kitchen remodel for a large new refrigerator and keep the old one until your budget permits replacement. Often a pro can help you prioritize.

Here are some items to consider for your wish lists.

There are many grades of cabinets and types of counters. Cabinets can be stock (made in typical sizes), semi-custom (a range of stock and special-made sizes) or custom. They can be domestic or imported. Customized insides can be purchased from the same manufacturer or from separate manufacturers (for example, the coated-wire cabinet inserts). Interiors can be particle-board or plywood, surfaced with wipe-clean plastic or varnished. At the low end, cabinets for a modest kitchen can range from $4000 to $7000. At the deluxe end, English-import kitchen cabinets can run up to $100,000.

Cabinet doors can have a variety of designs and shapes. Exterior materials can be wood, metal, laminate or composites with hand-applied or baked-on finishes. Cabinets can fit under soffits or go all of the way to the ceiling. Though 24-inch-deep bottom cabinets and 12- or 13-inch-deep top cabinets are standard, heights and depths can vary. Curves, bump-outs and angles are very popular.

Accessories can include custom pantry interiors, lazy-susans, pull-out shelves, pot-and-pan racks, silverware drawers, pop-up appliance cabinets, roll-out islands, towel bars and other "toys" that add to the cost.

Part of doing your remodeling homework is to start a clipping file of pictures of rooms you like from magazines. Think about colors and design details. Put your pictures away for awhile and take them out again. What is the same or different? Is there a consistent style? What details do you like? Your clipping file will aid you in assembling your project wish list.

If the project isn't finished, and you want to sell your home, the appraiser will use a contractor's rate to determine how much it will cost to complete what needs to be completed and subtract that amount from the market value of your home. The appraiser reasons that a buyer will deduct the amount needed to finish the house from its value or not purchase it. Your realtor may want to advertise your poorly remodeled home as one that "needs TLC" or as "a handy-man's special."

Seventy-four percent of the surveyed appraisers told *Practical*

DO YOUR HOMEWORK

You have a budget and you've figured out what the rules are. What's next?

Start a clipping file of pictures that you like from magazines. Think about colors and design details. Put your pictures away for awhile and then take them out to look at them. You will see them in a new light. What is the same or different about the pictures? Are they all of one style? Is the color the same? Are window configurations similar?

Make a wish list and prioritize it. What do you want most? What least? Sometimes you can stub-in

KITCHEN WISH LIST

The kitchen wish list probably requires the most choices and the most products.
Here is a list to help start your thinking process.

Do you want...?

Breakfast nook
Table eating area
Counter eating area
Planning desk
Laundry area
Walk-in pantry
Utility closet
Recycling center
Wine storage
Doors and pass-throughs to the outside
   (including French doors)
Windows (either bigger or special windows
   such as bays and skylights)
Built-in ovens
Commercial ranges (these are often much
   heavier than traditional household equip-
   ment and seldom have self-cleaning ovens)
Range hood
Second range or oven
Separate indoor barbecue grill
Warming drawer
Heating lamp
Warming shelf under range hood
Microwave
Second microwave
Built-in toaster
Built-in can opener
Built-in wrap and towel storage

Sink (single-, double-, triple-bowl with
   built-in cutting or drain boards)
Second sink
Hot-water dispenser
Soap and lotion dispensers
Garbage disposal
Faucets (some have built-in sprayer or tall
   goosenecks)
Trash compactor
Dishwasher
Second dishwasher
Refrigerator (either built-in or free-standing,
   residential or commercial)
Ice maker
Water cooler
Lighting (fluorescent, incandescent, halogen
   placed in the ceiling, the soffits, under
   cabinets)
Appliance garage
Electrical strips to plug in a variety of
   appliances
Built-in mixer storage
Hanging racks
Cabinets (either facelift or new)
Island in kitchen
Custom cabinet pull-outs, lazy-susans and
   racks
Counters
Floors

Counter surfaces include laminate (the least expensive), ceramic tile, Corian or other solid-surface material, butcher-block, marble or granite (the most expensive). You can use more than one in the same kitchen — such as a laminate counter and marble island. Counters can be of different heights and depths. Maybe you want a lower-height counter for children, or a marble-topped counter for rolling dough, or a baking center combining bins and counter.

Consider the cook. Perhaps the cook is taller or shorter and would be more comfortable working at counters that differ from standard height. Perhaps the cook has disabilities and needs to have a custom kitchen with such items as a lower

sink, shelf under the microwave or beside the oven.

There are also many choices in flooring. Indoor/outdoor carpet, vinyl, ceramic tile and wood are among the most common choices. Among more exotic choices are marble or French limestone.

Local suppliers can give you costs for your market on many of these materials.

Bathroom Wish List

For the bath there are the same types of choices in terms of cabinets, counters, flooring and accessories as for the kitchen. Some luxurious bathrooms feature marble or granite-tile floors and counters. The smaller space makes the selection of such materials

more economical — you don't need as much material as you do in the typical kitchen remodel.

You also need to decide if you want a separate shower, two vanities, or a whirlpool bathtub. Among more upscale choices for a typical bathroom remodel are the selection of a sauna, a steam room, a habitat room or a bidet.

For safety you can consider scald-guard faucets, non-slip surfaces or a guard over the tub spout (particularly useful if you have small children). For those who have difficulty walking or standing, you can install grab bars, blade-handled faucets (easy to turn on with the wrist) and other such accessibility and safety features.

If you are starting a bathroom

from scratch, you might well consider making it accessible. New products, such as brass-coated and colorful grab bars, have taken away the clinical appearance of accessible bathrooms. Truly accessible bathrooms have a five-foot-wide turning radius to accommodate wheelchairs. They also have such features as roll-in showers.

You can make your bathroom easier to use by installing a separate shower, giving generous clearances between fixtures and putting the supports in for grab bars to added later.

Family Room Wish List

There are lots of things to think about including in a family-room addition. You still need to think about cabinetry, walls and flooring materials. Other wish-list items can include:

Media center
Surround-sound stereo
Built-in bookshelves
Game area
Computer area
Fireplace
Wet bar
Indoor barbecue grill
Mini-kitchen
Built-in seating
Great room combined with kitchen
Eating area
Doors to the outside leading to a
    deck or patio

In addition to the top-three home improvements — kitchens, bathrooms and room additions — there is growing interest in home office space and in separate apartments within the home or attached to it.

Many families are looking for less expensive and more dignified ways to house aging parents. In some families, the children are unable to find jobs and leave the nest. These are perfect uses for an extra apartment. Zoning laws may dictate whether you can have a full kitchen or not. However, these added spaces, with or without a kitchen, provide privacy for the extended family.

As technology advances, home offices will become more common. If you plan a home office, provide

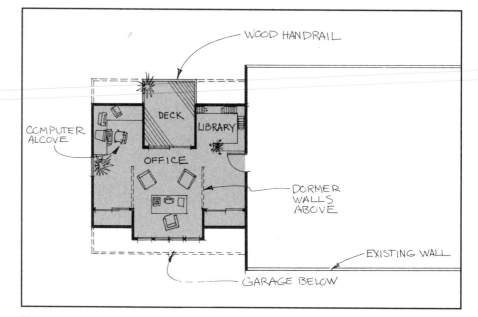

Home offices are becoming more popular. Plan R-120 (page 68) creatively converts unused space over the garage into a full office complete with computer center and library.

extra cooling — office equipment and lights generate heat. You will probably need to have room for not only a desk, bookshelves and a computer set-up, but also a FAX machine, copier and printer. Install heavier wiring and more outlets to handle all of the electronic equipment. Some home offices include television and stereo equipment, a sort of electronic cocoon.

One of the most important decisions affecting the success of your remodeling project will be who you select to make decisions. You can already see that there are lots of decisions to be made.

Decide who in your family will make the decisions. Either elect one member of the family as the primary decision-maker or make family decisions as a committee. Architects, professional builders and remodelers all over the country complain of being reluctant marriage counselors. They say that if one family member acquiesces on a point just to keep peace for the moment, it will haunt the project long after completion. Don't put yourself in the position of waking up every morning and saying to yourself, "I really wanted the white cabinets."

PICK YOUR PLAN

You have your budget, your list, your priorities and your decision maker. Now you can study our plans to see which one is right for you.

The best additions look like they have been there all along. One of the charms of older homes is that they evolve to fit family needs. Additions should fit that pattern.

Look at your roof shape, the type of exterior material on the existing house and the style of your windows. Your new addition should match or improve the spirit of your existing home.

If you have a two-story house, an addition either needs to be a two-story addition or be designed so that it won't obscure second-story windows.

Trellises, patios and decks can also link the old to the new. You will see that these are options in many of the plans featured. Once again, you can plan for trellises, patios and decks now, but add them when your budget permits.

You may find a plan that you really like, but the existing house shown with the plan doesn't look like your house. You can work with a local designer, architect or builder/

You probably won't get the best job if you use the old saying: "Get three estimates and pick the lowest price." Picking your remodeler is harder than that. You want to know that he or she delivers quality and value on schedule. You will need to do a lot of checking. Read contracts carefully. Pick a pro you feel comfortable with.

remodeler to adapt the plan. You can also customize your plan by using our exclusive Home Remodeler Service. (See page 110 for more details.)

PICK YOUR PRO

You should do it yourself only if you are a dedicated craftsman and can keep deadlines. Otherwise hire a pro.

Ask your friends for recommendations. Cream rises to the top and so do reliable pros. Two-thirds of the consumers surveyed for *Professional Builder & Remodeler* cited referrals from friends as the way they would choose a remodeler. The builders surveyed reported that more than 90 percent of their work was referrals from previous clients. Many builder/remodelers don't advertise. More than half of the builder/remodelers surveyed put signs on the lawn outside current jobs, 41 percent had listings in the yellow pages and 30 percent used newspaper ads.

Bryan Patchen, executive director of The National Association of Home Builders Remodelers Coun-

cil, says the oft-quoted "get three estimates; take the lowest bid" is not the way to proceed. You wouldn't choose a heart surgeon based on price. *Professional Builder & Remodeler's* survey ranks price third. Surveyed remodeling consumers value quality first and reliability second.

When you have your referrals ask questions. Did the homeowners feel comfortable with the remodeler? Could they communicate well? Did subcontractors show up on time? Did they clean up daily? Was the work done on time?

Find out how long the firms you are considering have been in business and if they have a permanent business address. Check with your local Better Business Bureau to see if there have been complaints. Some states also have business licensing offices where you can find out if an individual has operated under different names. Steer clear of firms that seem to stay in business only a short time under each business name or frequently file for bankruptcy.

Contact no more than five of the

firms you feel measure up. No pro likes to waste time on a potential client they feel might be bottom-fishing. Some remodelers will not competitively bid on jobs. Ask up front if they charge for estimates — some do, some don't.

When the remodeling pro visits your home, ask if they are licensed and offer warranties. Two-thirds of the pros *Professional Builder & Remodeler* surveyed do offer warranties on remodeling jobs. Also ask for proof of liability and workman's compensation insurance. You don't want to get stuck paying for worker injuries that might occur on your job.

Ask for the names and addresses of past customers and past subcontractors and suppliers. Contact them. You want to know not only if the customers are happy but also if subs and suppliers like working with the remodeler and if they get paid on time. There have been incidents where subcontractors or suppliers have put liens on remodeled homes because the contractor didn't pay them.

Avoid contractors for whom you can't verify licenses and insurance. Avoid high-pressure sales tactics and remodelers who promise a special deal because they'll use your house in their advertising. Most important of all, don't pay for the job in advance.

By now you can understand why price isn't your only consideration in a remodeling project. The cost of running a properly licensed and insured business will of course be higher than for someone who does not carry those professional burdens.

You don't want to make yourself liable for other builder/remodeler's problems or lose your home by dealing with someone unscrupulous. Hiring reliable builder/remodelers helps determine how long you'll be living with the mess of remodeling — and it is a mess! The level of quality delivered by the builder/remodeler is something you'll be living with long after you sign the last check. Do it right.

You should feel comfortable with the pro you pick. A remodeler who at first tops your list may not be the best choice for you. Not all people

During the remodel try to create a place of refuge in your home — a place away from the noise, turmoil, dirt and confusion — where you and your family can relax.

Schedule regular visits with your builder/remodeler to inspect the job. As work progresses, you may want to make changes. Regular site inspections make sure that the job progresses smoothly, the way you want it.

get along. Your builder/remodeler will practically become a member of the family while your project is under construction.

The pro you pick should provide you with a contract that you both sign and a written schedule for work and payment. Study the documents carefully. The contract legally binds both of you. The schedule is your timetable. Make sure that all of the materials are specified. If you are comparing estimates from several builder/remodelers, make sure that they cover all of the same items.

There are two kinds of contracts. In a flat-bid contract, the contractor gives a single price for the remodel with change orders extra. In a negotiated contract, the contractor agrees to do the work for time and materials not to exceed a certain price and a stated fee for his or her services. Sometimes the fee is a percentage of the remodel; other times it is a flat fee. The flat fee is better because the builder/remodeler knows up front what the fee is. There is no incentive to run up costs to increase the fee charged. If there are savings to be made in materials or labor, these are passed along to the consumer. Most contractors who work this type of negotiated contract bill monthly and include copies of invoices from suppliers and subs.

If you feel comfortable with the

builder/remodeler but find the estimate high, work with him or her. Perhaps you can change flooring to some other material than specified in the contract. Perhaps you can rough-plumb that bathroom and finish it when you have more money. Don't sacrifice job quality and cheat yourself at resale.

Pay attention to the timetable. Subs and suppliers need to have access to your home. If you aren't home and have made no plans to let a sub have access to the job, the sub will have to reschedule — that can take extra time and cost money. You also need to know when the power, gas or water will be off and how long you'll be without use of a kitchen sink.

There are some other issues you want to discuss up front and put in the contract. How often will the work area be cleaned? What size dumpster will be on the site and how often will it be emptied? Where will workers eat lunch? Where will they go to the bathroom? You may want to ask that a port-a-potty be brought to the job site. Each of these issues affects the cost of your job and your overall comfort level during the remodel.

If the remodeling is to be extensive, you will want to move out or seal up. You'll want to be dressed early in the morning. Contractors and subs often start at sun-up. It can be embarrassing to wander down to

the kitchen dressed in a ratty old robe and be met by a cheerful stranger wearing a hard hat and a tool belt!

During the remodel try to create a place of refuge within your home — a place away from the noise, turmoil, dirt and confusion. Also figure into your budget the cost of restaurant and carry-out meals. If the kitchen is being remodeled you may want to move crucial appliances into another room and set up a temporary kitchen.

Don't ask the subs questions about the job or over-socialize with them. They are there to do a specific job. The plumber can't be expected to know about the wiring, or the electrician know about the drywaller, and so forth. Your builder/remodeler has your contract, your budget, your drawings, your schedule, and is the only person who has the answers to your questions.

Schedule regular visits for you and your builder/remodeler to inspect the job. As work progresses, you may suddenly find that you just have to have a bay window in the breakfast nook for that perfect view of the bird feeder. It's OK to make changes. Regular site inspections with your pro will make sure that these can be done in a timely manner. Your pro will issue change orders which detail what the changes are and how much they will cost — this is why you set aside that extra 10 to 20 percent early in the budgeting process. Don't let change orders accumulate to be settled at the end of the job. Just as some people can get carried away with their credit cards and end up with surprising balances, you can get carried away with changes. Ten changes that each cost a couple hundred dollars will add up to $2000.

Depending on the length and scope of the job, payment can be made monthly or at certain specific times during the construction process. If you are doing a large project, you can have monies placed in a third-party escrow account to be paid out during the job. Discuss that with your builder/remodeler up front and spell it out in the contract.

Make sure that the builder/remodeler signs a lien release to protect you from subs and suppliers who file liens against your house in order to get paid. In some parts of the country, final payment can be delayed until there is proof that no such liens have been filed.

When your remodeling is finished, celebrate. Throw a party. Some builder/remodelers even share party expenses to show off their best work and yours. Enjoy your accomplishment and a job well done.

LET'S BUILD

You have your budget, plan, builder/remodeler, contract and schedule. Now it's time to make a mess.

No matter how carefully you try to protect your furnishings and separate the construction zone from the rest of the house, plan on dust. The fine dust of dry wall and plaster will work their way through even two layers of plastic. Clean often and well to keep the mess under control. If it is not in your remodeling contract, hire professionals to clean your whole house when the remodeling is complete.

You will need to select your building materials: flooring, cabinets, fixtures and other items on your wish list. Your builder/remodeler will give you a list and a timetable. The decision-maker or family committee needs to make all of the choices for materials and colors in a timely manner that will not hold up the job. Most building permits require building inspections at certain phases of construction. Walk the job with your builder/remodeler and the inspector to double-check proper workmanship and materials.

These inspection times may also be the right time for looking at unseen opportunities. Maybe you like the angles of the roof so much that you want a cathedral ceiling instead of a flat ceiling. Maybe you want to add a window or a skylight. Early on when the addition is framed is the least expensive time to make such changes. However, if you want to add something, talk to your builder/remodeler. Remember you added 10 to 20 percent of your budget just for such changes.

Despite all of the dust, noise and general inconvenience of having your home in turmoil, you will begin to see changes. Your plans will turn into reality, an exciting process.

With the final coat of paint and last clean-up you will begin to live in your "new" home. You won't be bumping your hip on that old kitchen counter. You won't be slip-sliding into the shower. Getting ready in the morning will be easier. You'll have your retreat or the kids will have theirs. In the end, it will all be worth it.

When the project is done, celebrate. Throw a party. Some builder/remodelers even share the expense of a party in order to show off their best work and yours. Enjoy your accomplishment and a job well done!

SIXTIES RANCH EXPANDS WITH FAMILY

Typical of the 60s, this ranch has a galley kitchen, dining "L" and small family room. The 90s solution provides a large family kitchen with informal eating area, plus a formal dining area divided from the new family room with a two-sided fireplace plus an optional deck.

Original Floor Plan

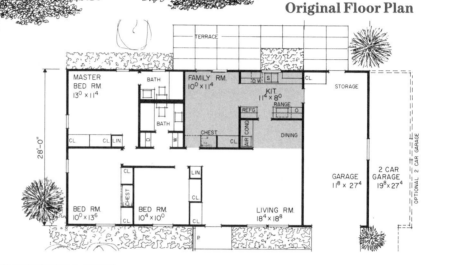

PROBLEM:

▲ Spaces are too small.

▲ Kitchen is cramped.

▲ There is no formal dining room.

▲ Flow from room to room is poor.

▲ Sight lines are bad (can see into kitchen from living room).

Remodeled Floor Plan

The former family room has become the dining room bracketed by half walls and columns. A two-sided fireplace divides the dining and family rooms. The addition includes the family room, part of the expanded kitchen, and a quarter-circle breakfast bay.

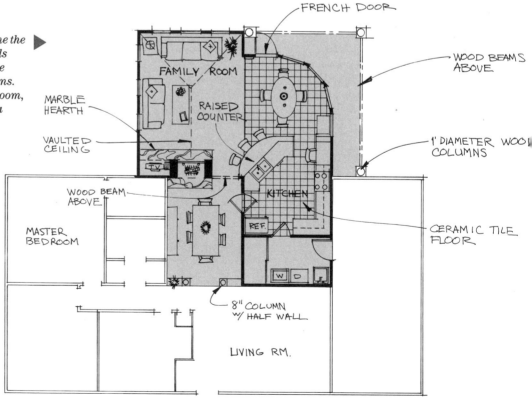

**Remodeling Plan
R100**

ARCHITECT'S VISION

The existing house is a collection of small rooms — none large enough for family interaction. Changing the relationship of existing rooms provides both formal entertainment and privacy for adults. The kitchen/family addition gives the family space to play.

SOLUTION:

▲ A new wall recasts the existing dining area into a laundry with direct access between the garage and kitchen.

▲ The kitchen expands into the addition. An angled peninsula adds counter space but keeps the cook part of family interaction.

▲ Former family room becomes the formal dining room.

▲ Dining and family rooms share the two-sided fireplace. The family-room side has a niche for large-screen television.

▲ Plan changes improve sight lines. From front door one sees through the dining room, past the fireplace, and out windows to backyard.

▲ *View from new family room looks towards double-sided fireplace that separates family room and formal dining room. Next to fireplace are built-ins for books and television. To the left is breakfast area and eating counter in kitchen.*

▼ *The addition has a simple hip roof that allows for a surprising amount of creativity inside. The breakfast bay is a quarter-circle of windows recessed inside the addition. This design allows the roof to protect the breakfast area from too much sun and also provides a pleasant wrap-around porch.*

To order construction drawings for this Remodeling Plan, see page 110.

TO ORDER BY PHONE CALL TOLL FREE 1-800-521-6797

KITCHEN ADDITION BALANCES TRI-LEVEL

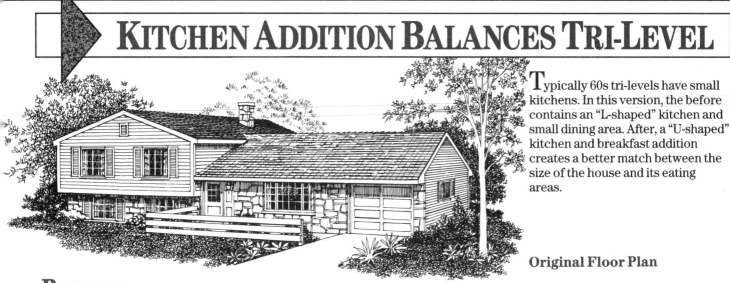

Typically 60s tri-levels have small kitchens. In this version, the before contains an "L-shaped" kitchen and small dining area. After, a "U-shaped" kitchen and breakfast addition creates a better match between the size of the house and its eating areas.

Original Floor Plan

PROBLEM:

▲ Kitchen is too small for house size.

▲ Counter space (only five feet) is inadequate.

▲ Dining area is cramped.

▲ May be hard to blend the variety of existing roof shapes.

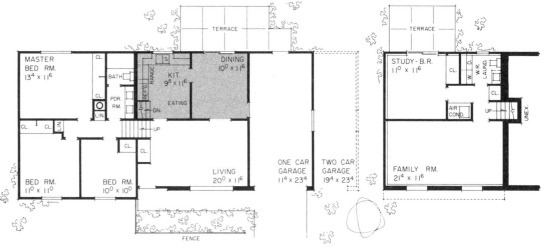

Remodeled Floor Plan

Room addition continues the theme of the multi-level plan. Old kitchen becomes the butler's pantry. New kitchen has more than three times the counter space of the old. New breakfast area steps down from the kitchen.

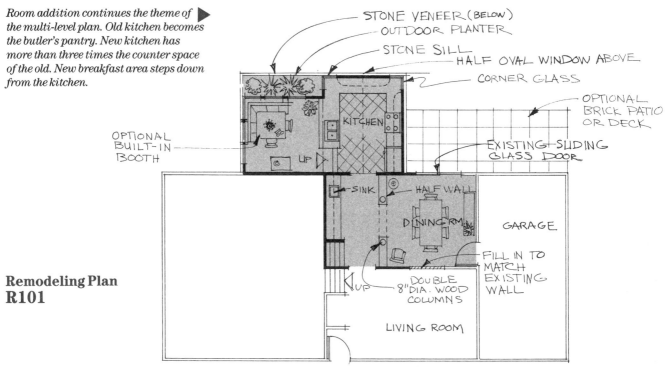

**Remodeling Plan
R101**

View from kitchen doorway looks over sink and into sunken breakfast area. Note wrap-around corner windows and fan-shaped clerestory window topping cabinets.

ARCHITECT'S VISION

*T*he challenges are to reorganize the informal and broken interior living spaces into useful formal spaces that match the size of the house and to coordinate the addition with existing wall and roof shapes. The kitchen/breakfast addition provides much needed kitchen and informal dining space.

SOLUTION:

▲ New "U-shaped" kitchen functions better and has three times the counter space including a length of six and one-half feet of unobstructed counter.

▲ Part of the original kitchen helps expand the small existing dining room into an inviting formal space. Columns separate the new dining room from the butler's pantry (also recycled from original kitchen).

▲ Light floods the breakfast nook. Six windows include one that wraps the corner.

▲ Careful scale and a variety of roof lines accent and soften the existing rear elevation's overall mass. Stone walls anchor addition.

▼ *A series of roof lines balances the addition and lessens the overwhelming mass of the existing house. Massive stone base also balances the existing house and anchors addition. The roof projects over breakfast area to shield the wrap-around windows.*

To order construction drawings for this Remodeling Plan, see page 110.

TO ORDER BY PHONE CALL TOLL FREE 1-800-521-6797

ADDED KITCHEN IMPROVES ON TRADITION

Though this traditional plan does have a formal dining room, the kitchen is very small and has no informal dining area. The addition enlarges the kitchen, links a new informal breakfast area with the existing family room and provides inviting patio space.

Original Floor Plan

PROBLEM:

▲ Kitchen is too small.

▲ Kitchen is isolated from family room.

▲ There is no informal eating area.

▲ Existing second story limits addition's height.

Remodeled Floor Plan

Modest-sized kitchen includes more than 20 feet of counter space and a cooking island. The new breakfast area is open to the family room. French doors lead from the breakfast room to the covered patio which is also accessible from the family room. ▶

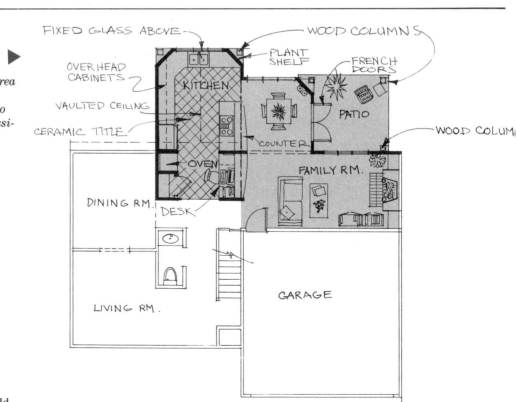

**Remodeling Plan
R102**

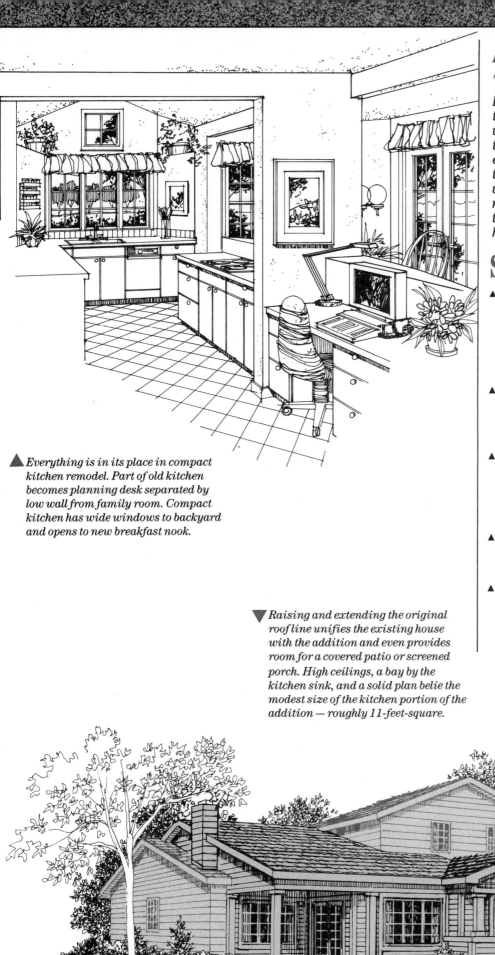

ARCHITECT'S VISION

*T*he kitchen expansion and new breakfast and patio spaces need to flow into what is already a very good basic plan. The addition of short walls within the existing house to frame in a pantry and a planning desk gives variety to existing plan flow. One may enter either the kitchen or the family room to reach the heart of the home.

SOLUTION:

▲ Adding the modest-sized addition increases the kitchen's size by almost 200 percent; 10-foot ceiling and sink bay make the 11-foot-wide kitchen seem larger.

▲ Double ovens, pantry and planning desk form a transition area between the existing house and the new addition.

▲ Breakfast area provides needed informal eating space and integrates existing family room and new kitchen into an informal living core.

▲ Covered patio improves overall plan flow and can become a screened porch.

▲ Raising and extending the original roof lines shelters the addition and blends it seamlessly with the existing house.

To order construction drawings for this Remodeling Plan, see page 110.

TO ORDER BY PHONE
CALL TOLL FREE
1-800-521-6797

▲ *Everything is in its place in compact kitchen remodel. Part of old kitchen becomes planning desk separated by low wall from family room. Compact kitchen has wide windows to backyard and opens to new breakfast nook.*

▼ *Raising and extending the original roof line unifies the existing house with the addition and even provides room for a covered patio or screened porch. High ceilings, a bay by the kitchen sink, and a solid plan belie the modest size of the kitchen portion of the addition — roughly 11-feet-square.*

CAPE-COD KITCHEN GROWS UP

The Cape Cod is a good, time-honored plan that is often a victim of the too-small kitchen syndrome. A kitchen/family addition strongly anchored by a large brick fireplace updates what is an otherwise functional plan.

Original Floor Plan

PROBLEM:

- ▲ Kitchen is tiny.
- ▲ The single dining space is very small.
- ▲ Steep gable roof combined with existing second-story shed roof make balance difficult.
- ▲ Second-story windows limit addition height.

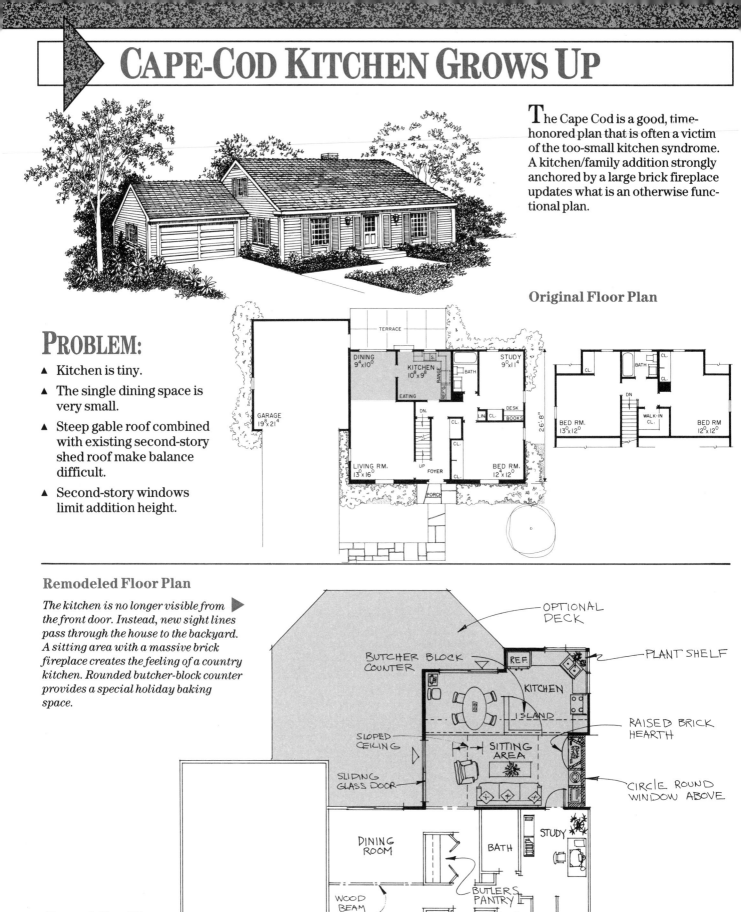

Remodeled Floor Plan

The kitchen is no longer visible from the front door. Instead, new sight lines pass through the house to the backyard. A sitting area with a massive brick fireplace creates the feeling of a country kitchen. Rounded butcher-block counter provides a special holiday baking space.

**Remodeling Plan
R103**

ARCHITECT'S VISION

*M*atching the rather plain existing rear elevation required careful selection of materials and balance of the low-slope, second-story shed roof with the overall steep pitch of the Cape Cod roof. Inside spaces must flow from existing rooms as well as improve overall sight lines through the house.

SOLUTION:

▲ Placing the kitchen on the outside corner of the addition takes it out of direct sight from the front door.

▲ The enlarged dining room now includes part of what was the original kitchen.

▲ A storage gallery, in space that was part of the original kitchen, links the existing house and the addition.

▲ A tiered roof slants from a 14-foot height to a seven-foot six-inch ceiling height and balances the addition and the existing house.

▲ Adding a sitting area dominated by a brick fireplace introduces a homey, country-kitchen feel.

▲ *Massive fireplace in sitting area hints at both the country keeping rooms and contemporary lifestyles. Stepped built-ins contain nooks for television, art books and wood.*

▼ *Large circular, porthole-like windows and a massive brick fireplace link new to old. Stepped roof balances dormer and steep-gabled roofs. Light also streams through two new gabled dormers.*

To order construction drawings for this Remodeling Plan, see page 110.

TO ORDER BY PHONE CALL TOLL FREE 1-800-521-6797

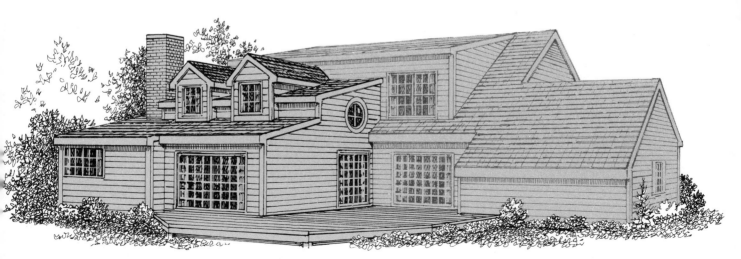

MODERN KITCHEN BUMPS OUT FRONT

Similar to many contemporary ranch homes of the 70s, the kitchen in this home is adjacent to the entry. The existing kitchen has inadequate food preparation areas and an uncomfortable dining area. The solution bumps out the entry side by eight feet to expand and improve both spaces.

PROBLEM:

▲ Food preparation area is insufficient.

▲ Dining area is cramped.

▲ There is no formal entry.

▲ Add-on to front elevation demands special care.

Original Floor Plan

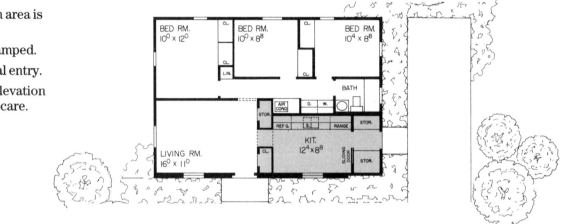

BED RM. 10⁰ x 12⁰
BED RM. 10⁰ x 8⁸
BED RM. 10⁴ x 8⁸
CL.
LIN.
BATH
AIR COND
D. W.
STOR.
REF G. S. RANGE STOR.
KIT. 12⁴ x 8⁸
SLIDING DOOR STOR.
CL.
LIVING RM. 16⁰ x 11⁰

Remodeling Plan
R104

Remodeled Floor Plan

▼ *Adding only 150 square feet completely changes both the feel of this kitchen/ dining space and nearly doubles its size. An island with eating bar illuminated by a skylight separates the dining and kitchen areas.*

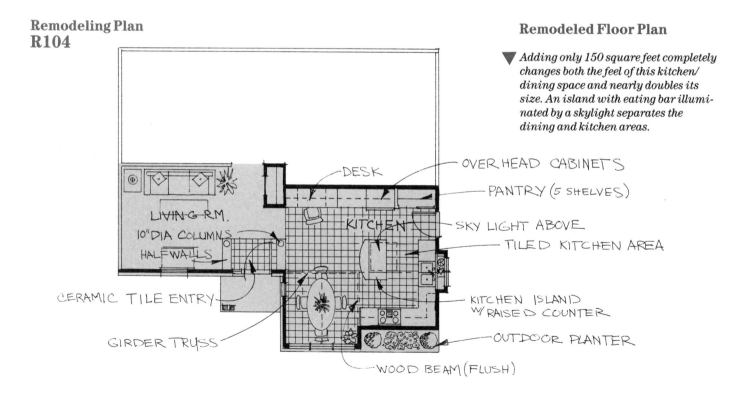

LIVING RM.
10"DIA COLUMNS
HALF WALLS
CERAMIC TILE ENTRY
GIRDER TRUSS
DESK
KITCHEN
WOOD BEAM (FLUSH)
OVERHEAD CABINETS
PANTRY (5 SHELVES)
SKY LIGHT ABOVE
TILED KITCHEN AREA
KITCHEN ISLAND W/RAISED COUNTER
OUTDOOR PLANTER

▲ *Expansion includes island kitchen and a lovely informal eating area. Note skylight over island and the cathedral ceiling and Palladian window in dining area.*

▼ *Three gables, a double-entry column and a contemporary-styled Palladian window are important design elements. These give the originally modest house a much stronger presence from the street. A plant shelf to the right of the dining bay softens the overall effect.*

ARCHITECT'S VISION

An addition to the street side of a house is both a challenge and an opportunity. The small addition balances the original design and transforms the character of the house. The newly added gable roofs give the ranch house a stronger presence from the street.

SOLUTION:

▲ Increasing counter space and adding an island vastly improves the amount of kitchen work area.

▲ A whole wall of storage includes a planning desk, refrigerator and pantry.

▲ Even though the new bumped-out dining area continues to be the only eating area, a contemporary-styled Palladian window gives it all of the class it needs to go formal.

▲ Columns both outside under new roof overhang and inside subtly define and establish a sense of entry.

▲ Varied roof lines, interesting window shapes and a variety of surface materials transform the home from blah to beautiful and enhance its curb appeal.

To order construction drawings for this Remodeling Plan, see page 110.

TO ORDER BY PHONE CALL TOLL FREE 1-800-521-6797

KITCHEN TAKES OVER EXISTING PORCH

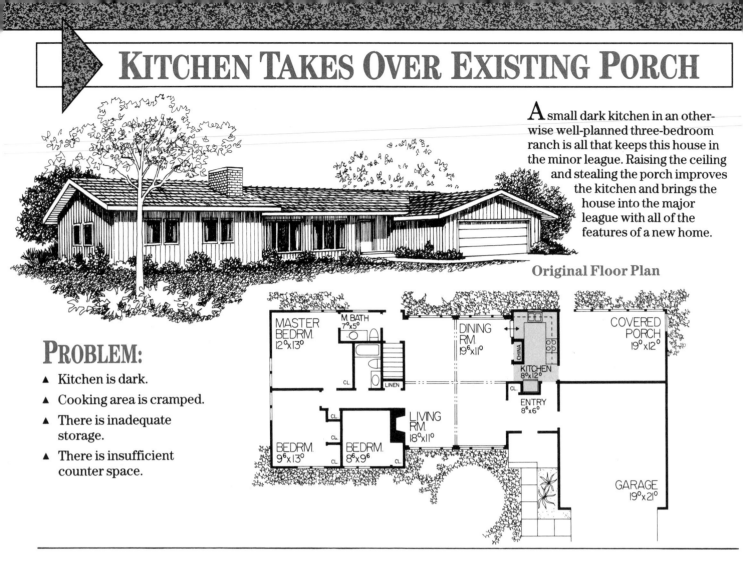

A small dark kitchen in an otherwise well-planned three-bedroom ranch is all that keeps this house in the minor league. Raising the ceiling and stealing the porch improves the kitchen and brings the house into the major league with all of the features of a new home.

Original Floor Plan

PROBLEM:

▲ Kitchen is dark.

▲ Cooking area is cramped.

▲ There is inadequate storage.

▲ There is insufficient counter space.

Remodeled Floor Plan

An existing covered porch provides space for expansion. Built-in ovens and a sink located in the new island make it much easier for two to cook. (See finished project on cover and page 5.)

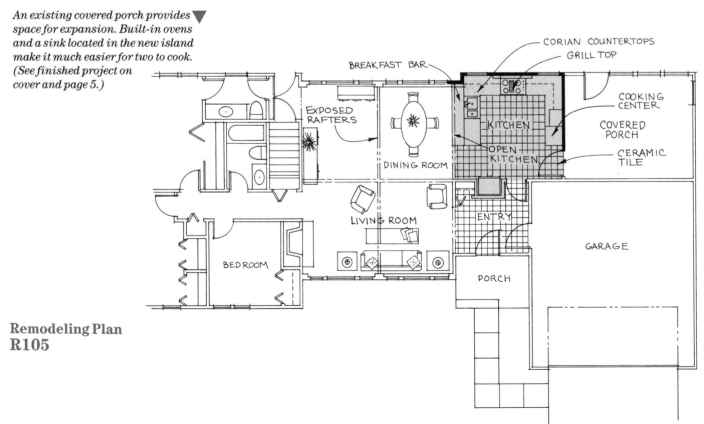

Remodeling Plan R105

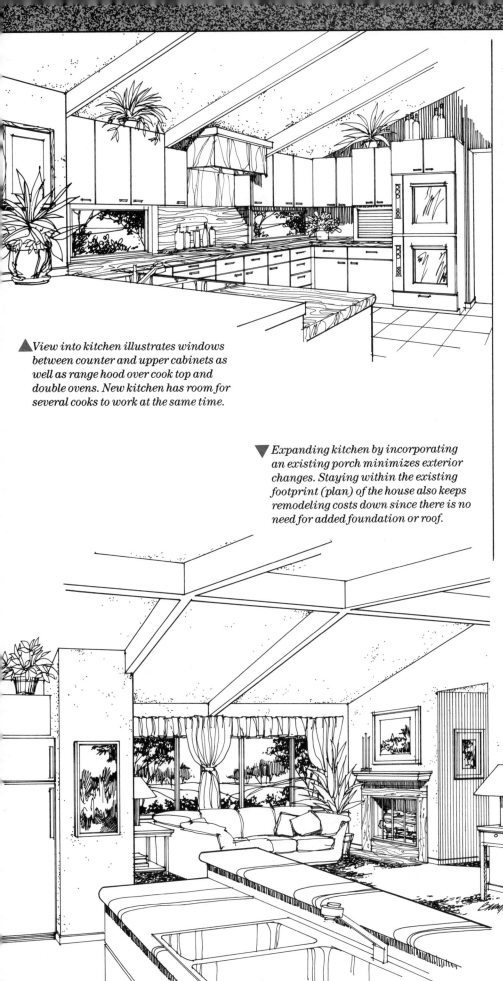

ARCHITECT'S VISION

Existing living and dining rooms have high-vaulted ceilings and exposed beams. In contrast, the former kitchen had a low, flat ceiling. Removing that ceiling and expanding into an existing covered porch matches the kitchen to the rest of the house.

SOLUTION:

▲ Removal of the flat ceiling exposes decking and beams giving kitchen more height.

▲ New counters add work space and improve kitchen work triangle.

▲ Windows between upper and lower cabinets offer a creative way to add light to a kitchen without sacrificing storage.

▲ Gourmet cook top and built-in ovens give the cook enough cooking and baking space to be creative.

▲ Expanding the kitchen through addition of existing porch space minimizes outside changes.

To order construction drawings for this Remodeling Plan, see page 110.

TO ORDER BY PHONE CALL TOLL FREE 1-800-521-6797

▲*View into kitchen illustrates windows between counter and upper cabinets as well as range hood over cook top and double ovens. New kitchen has room for several cooks to work at the same time.*

▼*Expanding kitchen by incorporating an existing porch minimizes exterior changes. Staying within the existing footprint (plan) of the house also keeps remodeling costs down since there is no need for added foundation or roof.*

FAMILY-ROOM ADDITION CHANGES FACE

Like many 60s ranches, this one has no family room. Adding a family room to the front of the house also makes room for a formal entry and gives the house a more inviting appearance from the street.

PROBLEM:

▲ Entry is part of the living room.

▲ There is no family room.

▲ Dining room is more like a hallway.

▲ Care must be taken not to harm the house's exterior character.

Original Floor Plan

Remodeled Floor Plan

The entry now reaches out to welcome visitors with room for a window seat and two coat closets. The family room is somewhat open to the kitchen through a window-like pass-through. The new eating area is part of the family room. By projecting forward toward the street, the addition also de-emphasizes the garage.

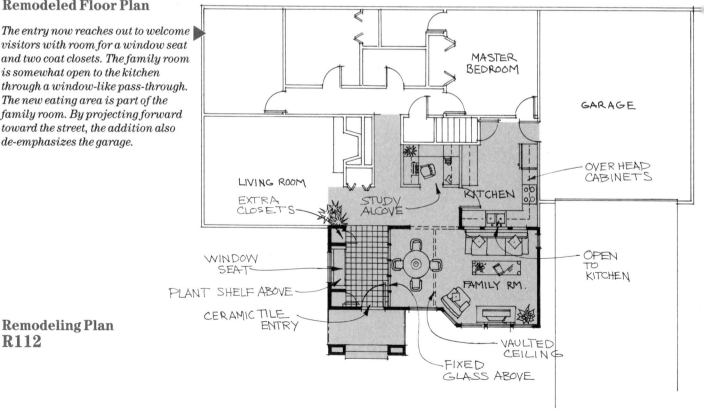

**Remodeling Plan
R112**

▲ *Light is key to success of family-room addition. Windows along left wall face street. Clerestory window mimics interior clerestory cut-out. Cut-out space on right adds light to kitchen. Square cut-outs send light from family room to entry.*

▼ *The gable-roofed portico provides a sheltered entry. Deep eaves projecting from the family-room gable provide variety and definition for the house as well as protection for the many windows.*

ARCHITECT'S VISION

*H*omes should have separate entry areas to welcome visitors and orient them to the rest of the home. The family-room addition both solves a family living problem and provides a sense of entry. The new entry is a prominent part of the streetscape that provides a sheltered transition between inside and out.

SOLUTION:

▲ The new formal entry hall with its window seats and closets allows the owners to greet guests and store coats before entering the rest of the house.

▲ The wall separating entry from the family room has five square windows above eye level that borrow light from the family room yet separate public and private spaces.

▲ The old dining room becomes a study/computer alcove next to the kitchen.

▲ The new dining area is much more inviting and doubles as extra family living space.

▲ Cut-outs in the former exterior wall lighten the interiors. Cut-outs on the inside wall are the same shape as high exterior windows. Kitchen cut-outs provide an inviting pass-through.

▲ The new front elevation has a strong and inviting street presence. The garage is now recessed. The entry is more inviting.

To order construction drawings for this Remodeling Plan, see page 110.

TO ORDER BY PHONE CALL TOLL FREE 1-800-521-6797

CLASSIC COLONIAL ADDS FAMILY SPACE

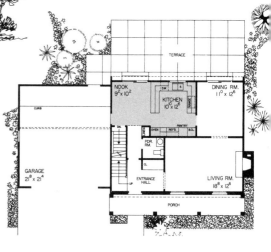

This classic center-entry Colonial lacks informal family living space. The family-room addition includes a breakfast nook for informal eating and an entertainment center. From the front door visitors see the inviting fireplace — the hearth that is important for any family home.

Original Floor Plan

PROBLEM:

- ▲ This four-bedroom house has no family room.
- ▲ Informal dining area is cramped.
- ▲ There is no informal place for the family to watch television.
- ▲ The back of the house has no design interest.

Remodeled Floor Plan

A barrel vault soars over the family room area. The vault is part of the library of classic elements that Colonial-style house remodels can draw upon for inspiration. The glass-filled arch at the end of the vault draws attention to its shape and fills the addition with light.

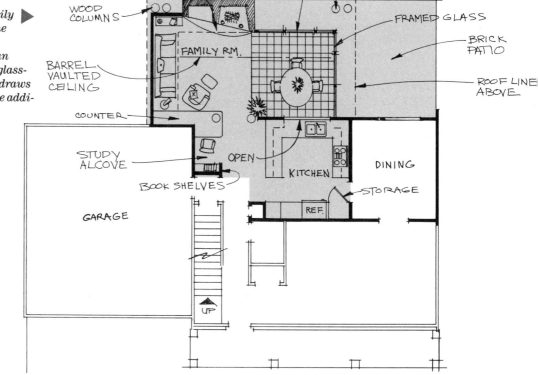

Remodeling Plan
R113

ARCHITECT'S VISION

*T*he formal proportions and details of the classic two-story Colonial call for similar detailing in the family-room addition. Classic inspiration can and should include light and volume. Attention should also be paid to the sight lines through the house from the front door.

SOLUTION:

▲ The family room provides ample informal living space.

▲ The classic barrel vault combines with clerestory windows in the end gable to give the addition both a classic and contemporary feel.

▲ A large informal breakfast nook lined with windows leads to a sheltered brick patio.

▲ Shelves and a long counter provide a study alcove for the children.

▲ Sight lines from the front door flow past a simple pair of columns and end in the quintessential sign of home — the classic brick fireplace in the family room.

▲ The fireplace includes an entertainment center.

▲ *Barrel-vaulted roof over addition gives classical appearance outside and contemporary appearance inside. Stepped fireplace has room for wood storage. Built-ins have space for television.*

▼ *From the outside, clerestory windows outline the metal-roofed barrel vault. The massive brick chimney solidly anchors the addition. Sturdy columns at the corners of the addition appear to support the roof.*

To order construction drawings for this Remodeling Plan, see page 110.

TO ORDER BY PHONE CALL TOLL FREE 1-800-521-6797

COZY FAMILY ROOM ADDS CHARM

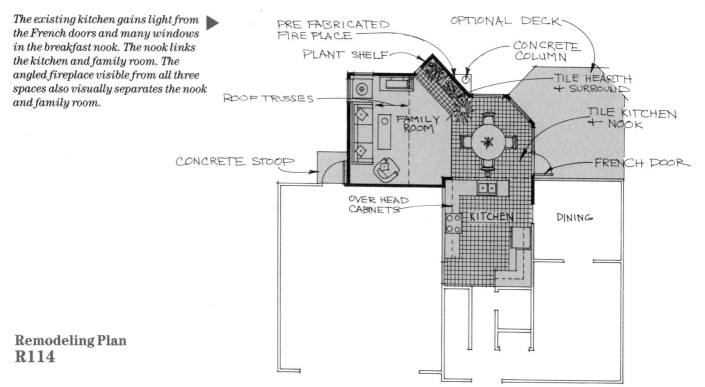

Like many older-style homes, this one lacks a family room. The new addition provides an informal eating area that links the existing kitchen to the family room and adds an inviting corner fireplace visible from all three spaces.

Original Floor Plan

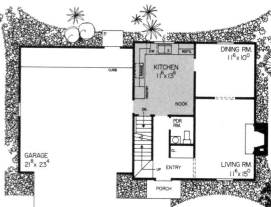

PROBLEM:

▲ Classic family home has no informal family area.

▲ Existing dining nook has no windows.

▲ Existing kitchen is dark.

▲ Addition must not obscure second-floor windows.

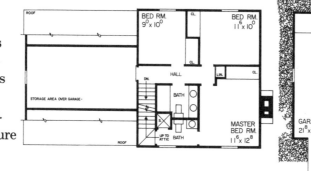

Remodeled Floor Plan

The existing kitchen gains light from the French doors and many windows in the breakfast nook. The nook links the kitchen and family room. The angled fireplace visible from all three spaces also visually separates the nook and family room.

**Remodeling Plan
R114**

▲ *From beamed breakfast nook, one sees tiled hearth and quarter-circle clerestory windows in new family room.*

▼ *The low sloped roof of the light-filled breakfast nook does not obscure upper bedroom windows. The family room, positioned behind the garage, soars uninhibited. The gable end features fan-shaped clerestory windows. Columns and wood trim highlight the addition.*

ARCHITECT'S VISION

*M*ajor volume in the new addition must be behind the garage in order to not block second-story windows. The challenge of volume results in a charming breakfast nook, strategically placed below the bedroom windows, that features a low sectioned roof similar to a bay window.

SOLUTION:

▲ Addition adds a light-filled, functional, informal family area.

▲ New dining nook has two sides of windows and a pair of French doors that lead to an optional deck.

▲ Opening the kitchen up to the light-filled nook brightens the kitchen.

▲ Placed behind the garage to avoid interfering with second-story windows, the high vaulted ceiling of the family room has a fan-shaped clerestory window in the gable end.

▲ The angled fireplace, visible from the kitchen, family room and nook, defines and separates these family living spaces.

▲ Exterior massing balances the tall family room behind the garage and the lower breakfast nook below second-story bedroom windows.

To order construction drawings for this Remodeling Plan, see page 110.

TO ORDER BY PHONE CALL TOLL FREE 1-800-521-6797

CLEVER EXPANSION BRIGHTENS HOME

This 1000-square-foot, modest ranch home has three bedrooms but no family room. The addition of a dining and family room as well as revamping the kitchen, substantially increases the overall square footage and improves traffic patterns through the existing living room.

Original Floor Plan

PROBLEM:

- ▲ Small ranch has no family room.
- ▲ Kitchen is too small.
- ▲ Cramped dining shares space with small kitchen.
- ▲ Existing traffic pattern cuts living room in two.

Remodeled Floor Plan

From tiny to terrific, the addition ▶ *transforms this cramped ranch house into a gracious family home. New kitchen within existing house opens to a large dining room. A two-sided fireplace and bar area separate the dining from the curved-wall family room.*

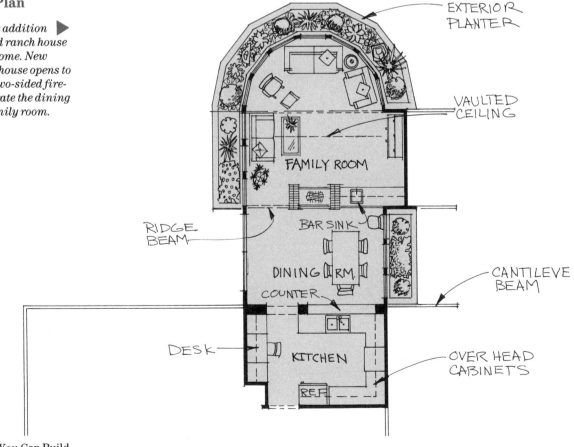

**Remodeling Plan
R115**

▲ *Ridge beam and fireplace divide new dining room and family room spaces. Windows in dining room follow roof pitch. Those in family room wrap around semi-circular addition. Built-ins are accessible from both spaces.*

ARCHITECT'S VISION

*R*anch houses call for long, low designs. For this addition, horizontal lines, low-pitched roof lines and deep eaves are reminiscent of Frank Lloyd Wright's Prairie School architecture. Such sophistication adds character to the existing simple house.

SOLUTION:

▲ Family-room addition adds more than 400 square feet to the 1000-square-foot existing house.

▲ New dining room allows expansion of the existing kitchen.

▲ Remodel of existing kitchen improves traffic flow through living room.

▲ Addition's open plan creates a large inviting space for entertaining.

▲ Two-sided fireplace and beverage bar separate the dining and family rooms.

▲ Windows that follow pitched roof line and semi-circular window wall add sophistication to the simple ranch.

▲ Planters outside blend the addition into site.

▼*Low roof shapes are in keeping with the low profile of the existing ranch house. The new roof undulates and unfolds into the semi-circular end wall of the family room. The sweep of windows in the family room and eight-foot-high windows in dining room literally flood the new space with light.*

To order construction drawings for this Remodeling Plan, see page 110.

TO ORDER BY PHONE CALL TOLL FREE 1-800-521-6797

COTTAGE RE-DO TRANSFORMS HOME

This two-story cottage has four large bedrooms, an eating area in the kitchen and a formal living room. By converting the existing kitchen into the formal dining room and adding new kitchen, breakfast and family rooms, the remodeled house has both formal and informal living spaces.

Original Floor Plan

PROBLEM:

▲ Kitchen is too small for a family-size, four-bedroom house.

▲ Single eating area is cramped.

▲ There is no family room.

▲ There is no room for a family media center.

Remodeled Floor Plan

New kitchen has plenty of counter space as well as an island with an eating counter and cook top. One wall of the breakfast area contains plenty of storage and a planning desk. The family room has a niche for the media center next to the fireplace. ▶

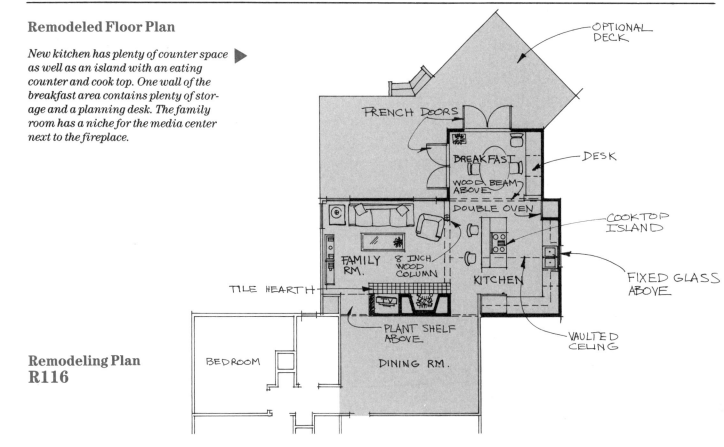

Remodeling Plan R116

▲ *Plant shelf over entry (far right) is part of the sculptural design in fireplace/ television wall. Past column and under arch is island kitchen.*

ARCHITECT'S VISION

The classic cottages of suburbia have a quaint, inviting look. Any addition should tastefully blend the existing style of mixed dormer and gable roofs. Mixing roof lines maintains the informal feel of the cottage but provides needed extra space.

SOLUTION:

▲ New kitchen features ample counter space, an eating bar and all of the other tools to feed the family that lives in a four-bedroom house.

▲ Existing kitchen and dining area are revamped into a single formal dining space.

▲ Informal dining in a breakfast nook off the kitchen leads to a deck.

▲ Breakfast nook has needed extra storage along one wall and a planning desk.

▲ The 13-foot-high family room ceiling uses a double tier of standard windows to bring in light.

▲ Outside, the family-room addition follows existing dormer roof. Breakfast room and kitchen blend with home's other gable roofs.

To order construction drawings for this Remodeling Plan, see page 110.

TO ORDER BY PHONE CALL TOLL FREE 1-800-521-6797

▼ *The kitchen/breakfast/family room addition maintains the character of the existing cottage but vastly expands its family space. The roof line of existing dormer extends over the high ceiling of the family room. A separate gable houses the kitchen and breakfast room.*

DUTCH-COLONIAL STYLE RENEWS HOME

This ranch has large rooms, but no family room. The garage and dining room box the kitchen in and make it seem dark. The addition bumps out the side of the house, brightening the kitchen and adding informal eating and family-room space.

Original Floor Plan

PROBLEM:

- ▲ Kitchen boxed in by garage is too dark.
- ▲ There is no informal eating area.
- ▲ There is no informal family living space.
- ▲ Design should minimize side-yard intrusion.

Remodeled Floor Plan

The new family room and breakfast area open off the kitchen. The space flows into a covered porch which adds interest to the front elevation. It also flows out the back towards a new back-yard patio.

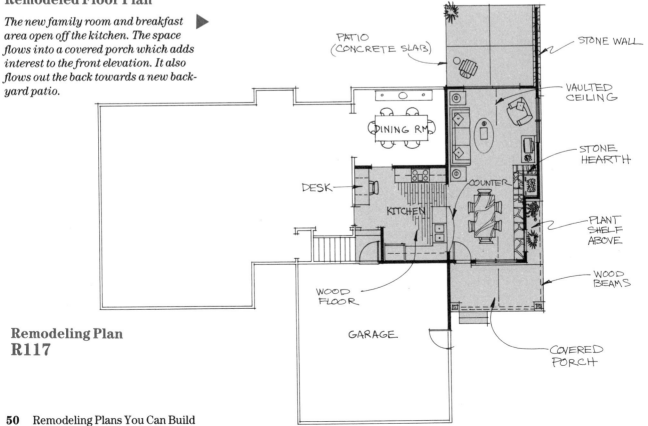

Remodeling Plan
R117

Architect's Vision

A *contemporary-styled addition, combined with historic design elements of the Dutch Colonial home, provides a new design that still reflects the comforting traditions of family living.*

Solution:

▲ Opening the kitchen to the bright family and breakfast spaces makes the kitchen seem larger and chases away darkness.

▲ Informal eating area leads to sheltered porch.

▲ Raised stone hearth defines and separates family and breakfast areas.

▲ Tile hearth surround, placement of square windows and exterior's board-and-batten siding and stone walls recall Dutch Colonial designs.

▲ Designed with a stone veneer exterior, the remodel gives stronger presence to the side elevation.

▲ Addition's width (13' 4") minimizes side-yard intrusion.

▲ Stone veneer extends line of gable roof to form a garden wall that shields new patio from neighbors.

▲ *Massive stone wall faces neighbors and provides a private garden wall for the backyard patio. A front covered porch adds light and space to the front of the breakfast nook. The stone garden wall extends privacy to the backyard patio.*

To order construction drawings for this Remodeling Plan, see page 110.

TO ORDER BY PHONE CALL TOLL FREE 1-800-521-6797

▼ *Only change to the front elevation from this view is stone veneer siding to match that of addition. Addition is in side yard on other end of garage.*

CARRIAGE-HOUSE IS NEW MASTER SUITE

The classic colonial-style home has always had wide appeal, yet such houses often have small or inadequate master suites. This remodeling solution includes an expansion of the existing dining room and the addition of a carefully scaled, first-floor master suite reminiscent of a romantic carriage house on a country estate.

PROBLEM:

▲ Master bathroom is too small.

▲ Closets are inadequate.

▲ Dining room is cramped.

▲ Addition should minimize intrusion into yard spaces and blend with the existing home.

Original Floor Plan

Remodeled Floor Plan

The expanded dining room leads into the separate world of the master suite. The vaulted bedroom ceiling slopes toward the bumped-out whirlpool bathtub. A private toilet compartment and a large separate shower maintain privacy in the otherwise open plan.

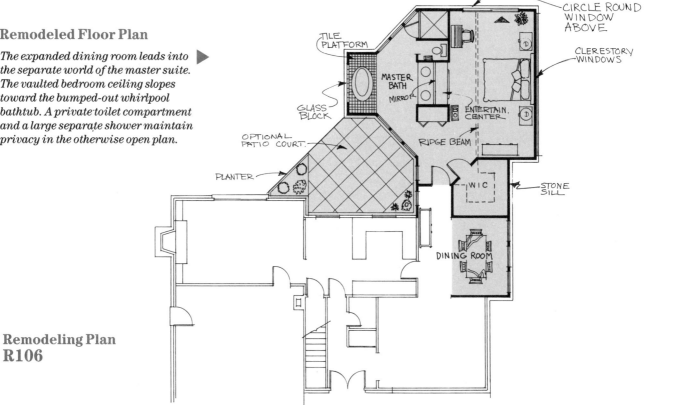

Remodeling Plan
R106

The addition to the rear of the house conjures images of the carriage house of old. The master-suite addition needs to stand tall in order to balance the two-story house with the one-story addition.

SOLUTION:

▲ From the kitchen, there is a pleasant view of the addition, designed to have the feeling of a carriage house.

▲ The dining room expands into the side yard and connects the existing house and the addition.

▲ A courtyard between the house and the addition provides a private family space.

▲ A recessed entry separates the master-suite addition from the dining-room expansion. Access to the addition is only for those who have the key.

▲ To maintain privacy, high clerestory windows face the neighbors; the bathroom faces the yard. Light pours in from the clerestory windows over the bed. A high round window provides views of the stars.

▲ The master suite contains a whirlpool bathtub and a four-foot-square shower for two.

▲

The romantic carriage house lives again in a private master suite. Clerestory windows flood the addition with light but protect the interior from neighbors' view.

◄ *View windows face yard interior rather than neighbors. Bump out uses glass block to maintain privacy in the bathtub.*

▼ *Bathtub nook has glass-block window topped by a clerestory to protect privacy. Shower opens on picture window that faces into yard.*

To order construction drawings for this Remodeling Plan, see page 110.

TO ORDER BY PHONE CALL TOLL FREE 1-800-521-6797

OPEN-PLAN MASTER KINDLES ROMANCE

Typically, older ranch houses have small master bedrooms and small inadequate master baths. There is often no privacy for the master suite. Windows are usually quite small. This master bedroom and bathroom addition provides design excitement, light, privacy and space.

Original Floor Plan

PROBLEM:

▲ Master bedroom is too small.

▲ Master bathroom is cramped and has no separate shower and bathtub.

▲ Windows are insufficient in number and inadequate in size.

▲ There is no separation of the master suite from other living spaces.

▲ There is no privacy.

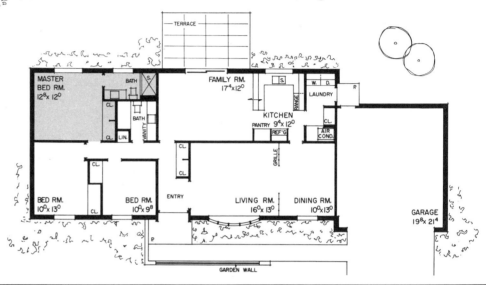

Remodeled Floor Plan

Vaulted ceilings, a whirlpool bathtub and a fireplace offer comfort and drama for this new master suite — where there is room for everything and everything has its place.

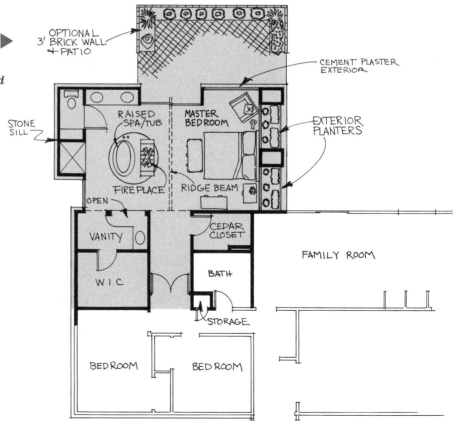

**Remodeling Plan
R107**

ARCHITECT'S VISION

Couples usually share the master bedroom. A shared master suite can be open and spacious rather than closed and compartmentalized. This master suite celebrates the grandeur of open space.

SOLUTION:

▲ Exterior planters surround the master-suite addition and provide the necessary privacy that allows the plan to be open.

▲ The existing master bedroom becomes a closet space including a cedar closet for seasonal storage.

▲ The master suite features an open plan for the couples who like everything in view.

▲ A sunburst window provides needed brightness and illumination for the open plan.

▲ A raised circular platform forms a pedestal for a spa bathtub and fireplace. The platform serves as a room divider and zones the suite into separate sleeping and bathing areas.

▲ Special details include a custom sit-down makeup area just for her.

▲ *Towering two-sided fireplace separates romantic spa bathtub from the master bedroom. Raised hearth is easily seen from the bathtub or the bed.*

▼ *The roof's prow extends into the backyard and shields the sunburst window. Recessed windows in the sitting and sleeping areas let in light without letting in the heat of the harsh summer sun. In the winter, these same windows welcome the warmth of the winter sun.*

To order construction drawings for this Remodeling Plan, see page 110.

TO ORDER BY PHONE CALL TOLL FREE 1-800-521-6797

SMALL ADDITION REVITALIZES MASTER

By 90s standards, this 60s ranch doesn't measure up in the master-suite department. The addition adds all of the features that newer homes have as standard: a sitting area, spa tub, separate shower, two lavatories, and a walk-in closet.

PROBLEM:

▲ Master bedroom is too small.

▲ Master bathroom is deficient by today's standards.

▲ Flow between walk-in closet and bath area is poor.

▲ The existing space is bland and lacks style.

Original Floor Plan

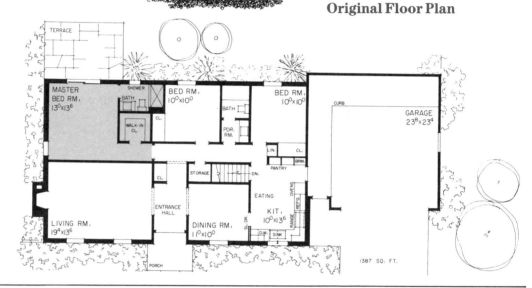

Remodeled Floor Plan

Adding only a little more than 10 feet to part of the rear of the house brings the master suite into the 90s. The new suite boasts a secret garden, a private sitting area, a large walk-in closet and a perfectly outfitted master bathroom.

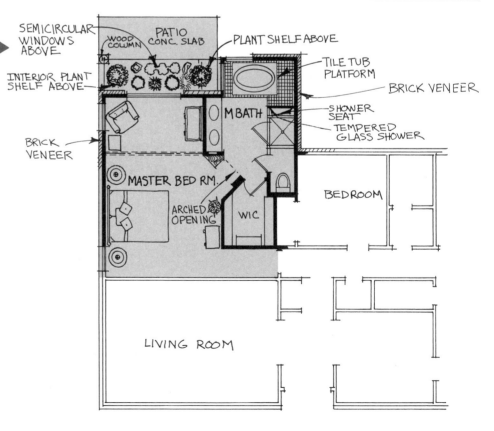

**Remodeling Plan
R108**

ARCHITECT'S VISION

There is nothing wrong with a simple design. The Shakers perfected classic, functional simplicity generations ago. The task here is to add on to the house in a way that balances the existing design with one that adds light and style to the master suite.

SOLUTION:

▲ The addition adds a sitting area to the bedroom space enhanced by a fan-shaped clerestory window and plant shelves.

▲ A bumped-out niche forms the platform for a spa bathtub and the seat in the all-glass shower.

▲ Two lavatories and a separate toilet compartment complete bathroom upgrades.

▲ Re-orienting the walk-in closet towards the new bathroom improves the flow between spaces.

▲ The new bathroom shields the private master patio from view from the rest of the house.

To order construction drawings for this Remodeling Plan, see page 110.

TO ORDER BY PHONE CALL TOLL FREE 1-800-521-6797

▲ *In only 10 feet, the addition provides a modern master bathroom. Platform of spa bathtub provides seat in the separate shower.*

▼ *The new gable roof of the addition blends into the gable roof of the main house. Only from the rear elevation are the changes to the home obvious. The clerestory fan-shaped window and the column supporting the porch add style without overpowering the rest of the house.*

MASSIVE MASTER-WING BLENDS IN

Cape Cod-style homes are frequently on large lots in established neighborhoods. Such houses make perfect starter homes that can grow with families. This dream master-suite addition even includes a mini-kitchen in the sitting room.

Original Floor Plan

PROBLEM:

▲ Growing family needs more bedroom space.

▲ There is no get-away space for parents of a growing family.

▲ Closet space is insufficient.

▲ A large one-story addition for a one-and-one-half-story house represents a design challenge.

Remodeled Floor Plan

Located off the living room, the new master suite is almost a get-away apartment. From the living room, a glass-block wall leads to a pair of French doors that open into a private sitting room. The sitting room has a mini-kitchen with under-counter refrigerator and sink as well as a three-sided fireplace.

**Remodeling Plan
R109**

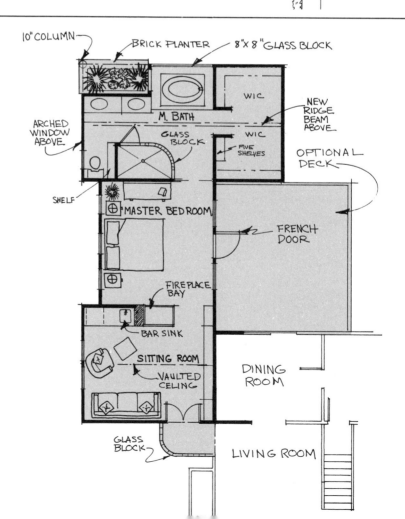

Curved glass-block wall gives large shower style and light and balances glass-block wall along bathtub platform. Pot shelf over double vanity houses light fixture. Bathtub window faces planter.

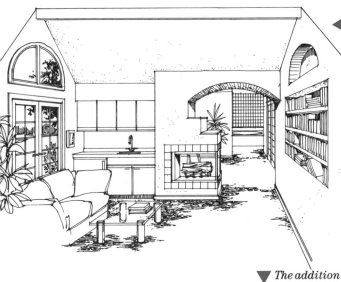

Seen from the other side, the bathroom wing creates a private space in which to nestle a deck. Large windows and door are in the master bedroom area.

The addition with its three gables defining the three private master-suite spaces also gracefully enhances the charm of the classic Cape Cod-style house. High ceilings within the addition help keep scale with the one-and-one-half- story existing home.

ARCHITECT'S VISION

A new addition, no matter how grand inside, should not compete with the quaint charm of the traditional Cape Cod home. The large, three-room addition needs to complement rather than overpower the existing home. The master-suite interior incorporates many luxury features.

SOLUTION:

▲ First-floor master suite is a boon to both growing families and those with empty nests.

▲ A separate entry gives the master suite great privacy.

▲ The sitting room pampers residents with built-in bookshelves, a three-sided fireplace, and a mini-kitchen complete with under-counter refrigerator and bar sink.

▲ His and hers closets provide ample storage.

▲ Clerestory windows protect privacy in the bedroom. French doors on the yard side can lead to a patio or deck.

▲ Fan-shaped windows in the sitting room and master bathroom let in light without infringing privacy.

▲ A two-person shower with a curved glass-block wall provides privacy for the toilet.

▲ Three gables clearly define the master bathroom, the bedroom and the sitting room, yet link the scale of the addition to that of the main house.

To order construction drawings for this Remodeling Plan, see page 110.

TO ORDER BY PHONE CALL TOLL FREE 1-800-521-6797

TOPPING GARAGE PROVIDES MASTER

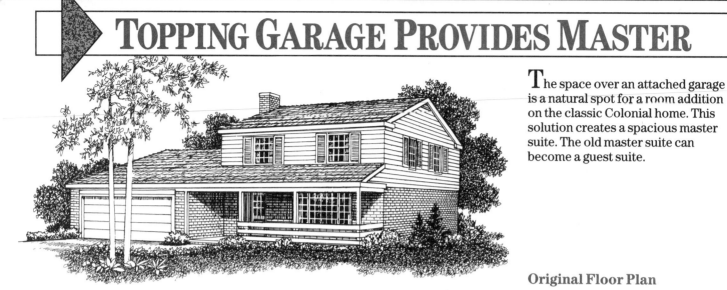

The space over an attached garage is a natural spot for a room addition on the classic Colonial home. This solution creates a spacious master suite. The old master suite can become a guest suite.

PROBLEM:

▲ Colonial home has three bedrooms.

▲ Existing master suite is short on closet space.

▲ Existing master bathroom is functional but not fashionable.

▲ Second-story addition will be a prominent street feature and needs to match and enhance home's style.

Original Floor Plan

Remodeled Floor Plan

Door to the suite opens to view the glass-block wall that provides privacy for the whirlpool bathtub. Other bathroom accoutrements include an 11-foot-long double vanity and a three-foot-wide shower door. A classic Palladian box-bay window provides plenty of interior light for the bedroom.

Remodeling Plan
R110

HALF ROUND WINDOW ABOVE (FIXED)

WHIRLPOOL BATH

8" LAP SIDING (MATCH EXISTING)

GARAGE ROOF

WIC

BATH BATH

BEDROOM

TILE PLATFORM

RIDGE BEAM ABOVE

GLASS BLOCK

SLOPED CEILING

LAM. COUNTER

EXISTING STAIRWELL

4 SHELVES

BEDROOM

BEDROOM

8" COLUMNS

Curved glass-block wall separates shower compartment and bathtub area from the main master bedroom area. Pot shelf is also light fixture over double vanity.

View from master bathroom, highlights dormer with its Palladian window and built-ins, perfect for books and television.

Classic Palladian window matches the detailing used in Colonial-style houses. Many will be surprised to find that the master suite is an addition.

ARCHITECT'S VISION

*T*he plan of the first-floor garage sets the limits for the space available upstairs in the master suite. The addition also needs to balance and complement the existing house. With such strict design parameters, the challenge is to make the outside interesting and the inside a surprise.

SOLUTION:

▲ The addition above the garage adds significantly to the home's overall square footage and provides a fourth bedroom.

▲ Generous walk-in closet space as well as an 11-foot-long double vanity and a television/stereo entertainment area in the bedroom expand storage space.

▲ Whirlpool bathtub wrapped in glass block is a sensual yet practical design feature.

▲ Separate shower, compartmented toilet and double lavatories with wall-to-wall mirrors meet the luxury and space standards set by new-home construction.

▲ Classical Palladian window fills the projecting dormer on the front elevation. Columns add another classic touch that links the addition's style with that of the Colonial-styled home.

To order construction drawings for this Remodeling Plan, see page 110.

TO ORDER BY PHONE CALL TOLL FREE 1-800-521-6797

MASTER ADD-ON BALANCES SPLIT-LEVEL

Many split-level homes, like this one, can be perfect family homes with the addition of a master suite. This home has three bedrooms and only one bathroom. The solution divides the home into parent and child areas. The existing bedroom becomes a sitting room and the entry to the new master suite.

Original Floor Plan

PROBLEM:

▲ Lack of master bedroom with its extra bath keeps home from meeting family needs.

▲ Master bedroom is too small.

▲ One bathroom must serve all family needs.

▲ There are few closets.

▲ It may be difficult to integrate addition with various house levels.

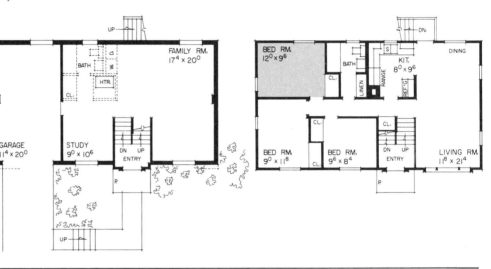

Remodeled Floor Plan

The old bedroom takes on new life as a ▶ *sitting room and transition space into the master suite. Down three steps from the other bedrooms, the master addition includes a mini-kitchen, walk-in closet and a luxurious master bathroom.*

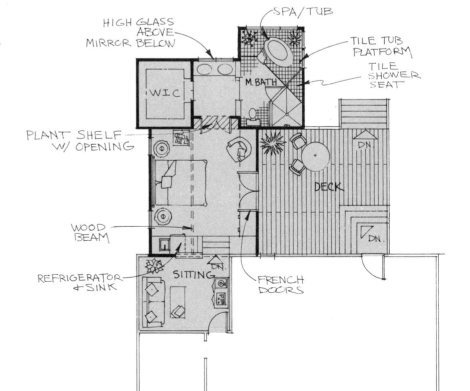

**Remodeling Plan
R111**

French doors on left lead to new deck; steps connect new master suite to original bedroom, now sitting area.

Looking from the master bedroom into the master bath, one sees the angled bathtub platform and the separate shower. Note how clerestory windows over the double vanity let in light yet maintain privacy.

The new addition brings the rear of the house back down to ground level. It also provides privacy for a deck area. Note that the addition, built over a crawl space, is a transitional level—not as high as the bedroom area or as low as the main living area.

ARCHITECT'S VISION

*T*he typical American split level looks like a foundation wall half out of the ground with a house on top. Though often awkward-looking from the outside, inside there is good family living space. The master-suite addition brings the overall house into balance and adds the bedroom and bath space such homes need.

SOLUTION:

▲ New master bathroom provides separate bathing and grooming areas to ease the morning rush.

▲ Existing bedroom becomes a sitting room that overlooks the new suite—which is two feet below the sitting room.

▲ The stair wall, cut out to open views between the sitting and bedrooms, also provides room for a mini-kitchen and a television entertainment center.

▲ High windows provide privacy and draw the eye to addition's vaulted ceilings.

▲ The double vanity is in a separate area from the rest of the bath; thus the shower will not steam up the vanity mirror.

▲ Windows surround the corner whirlpool. The bathtub platform also provides a seat for the large, all-glass shower.

▲ The addition helps anchor and balance the existing, raised level of the house.

**TO ORDER BY PHONE
CALL TOLL FREE
1-800-521-6797**
To order construction drawings for this Remodeling Plan, see page 110.

GARAGE CONVERTS TO FAMILY APARTMENT

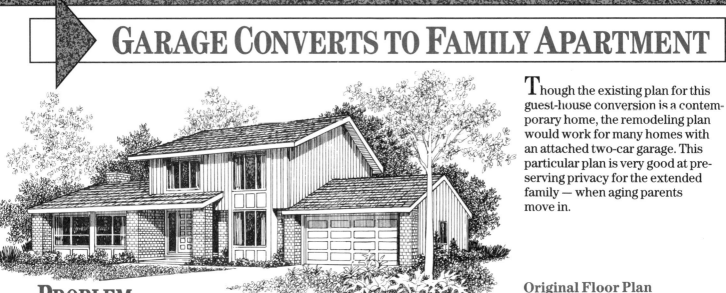

Though the existing plan for this guest-house conversion is a contemporary home, the remodeling plan would work for many homes with an attached two-car garage. This particular plan is very good at preserving privacy for the extended family — when aging parents move in.

PROBLEM:

- ▲ Mom and Dad need assisted living. Nursing homes are expensive and impersonal.

- ▲ Self-sufficiency and self-esteem are important concerns.

- ▲ Tensions run high when two families share living space.

- ▲ Privacy is an important concern for both parents and children, especially when schedules and living habits differ.

Original Floor Plan

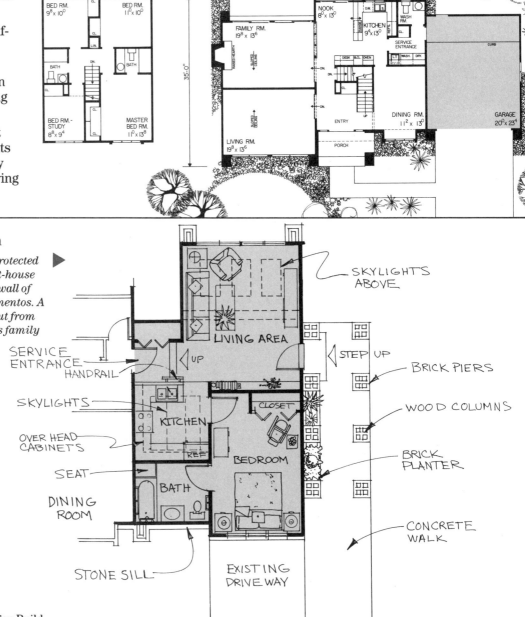

Remodeled Floor Plan

The covered porch provides protected access to the side-entry, guest-house entrance. Behind the door, a wall of shelving holds cherished mementos. A bright living area, bumped out from the original garage, overlooks family gardens.

**Remodeling Plan
R118**

ARCHITECT'S VISION

As the cost of retirement and nursing homes rise, families are searching for less costly and more personal alternatives to care for aging parents. This remodel of a two-car garage into a guest house provides private living space with its own outside entry.

SOLUTION:

▲ The two-car garage becomes the base for a spacious attached guest house.

▲ A covered walkway leads to a side entrance. This solution maintains the dominance of the home's main entrance without confusing visitors.

▲ New living area added onto garage faces backyard gardens.

▲ Attached entry to main house, kitchen and bath serve as sound buffers to minimize noise between dwellings.

▲ Full kitchen provides sense of independence, even if parents frequently dine with the rest of the family.

▲ Oversized bathroom has grab bars for safety and can be made wheelchair accessible.

▲ Bedroom on outside walls is distant from main-house noise.

To order construction drawings for this Remodeling Plan, see page 110.

**TO ORDER BY PHONE
CALL TOLL FREE
1-800-521-6797**

▲ *Two entries provide safety and privacy. Parents have easy access to the main-house and a private entry to the out-doors. The guest house also contains a complete kitchen and an oversize bathroom that can be adapted for wheelchair use.*

▲ *Entry from main house leads past coat closet into living room. Full kitchen provides option for private dining.*

SECOND STORY ADDS FAMILY MEDIA ROOM

Sometimes the only way to go is up. This ranch home has nice-sized rooms but no place to put a family media room. This second-story expansion has plenty of room for the media equipment and a big-screen television, as well as space for lots of storage.

Original Floor Plan

PROBLEM:

- ▲ Existing houses seldom have space for high-tech media rooms.
- ▲ Big-screen televisions are very large.
- ▲ High-tech systems need outlets and cable hook-ups.
- ▲ Media rooms need controlled lighting.

Remodeled Floor Plan

New stairs lead to a second-floor media room. The curved glass-block wall provides a moderate level of illumination during the day. The room features an entertainment center with plenty of room for the extra speakers in surround-sound systems.

Remodeling Plan
R119

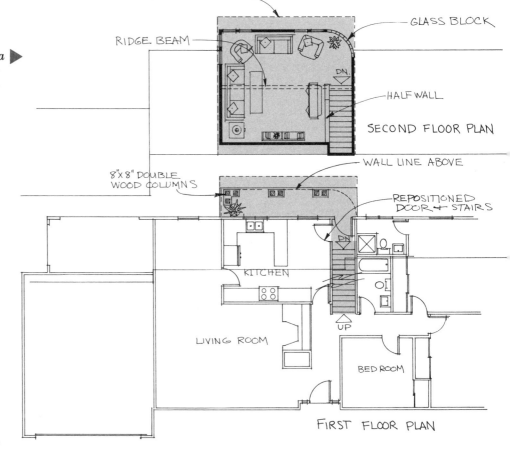

ARCHITECT'S VISION

Media rooms require controlled light and sound. Designing this media center as a loft retreat over the rear of a 70-foot-long ranch home gives it the privacy and seclusion of a theatre.

SOLUTION:

▲ Entry to the second-floor media room is from a new stairway added over the existing basement stairs.

▲ Custom media center has room for a large-screen television, VCR, laser disk, stereo and other high-tech toys.

▲ The design lends itself to including extra speakers for surround-sound systems.

▲ Window placement lets in light but does not cause unwanted reflection on the television screen.

▲ From the street, the addition extends the roof; from the backyard, the addition projects from the existing wall of the house and provides space for a covered rear porch.

▲ *Focus is on the techie-toys of entertainment; built-ins provide room for large-screen television, VCR, speakers and other elements for the perfect media room.*

▼ *The contemporary curved glass-block wall at the top of the stairs is the first clue that this addition is a high-tech entertainment space.*

To order construction drawings for this Remodeling Plan, see page 110.

TO ORDER BY PHONE CALL TOLL FREE 1-800-521-6797

TOPPING GARAGE ADDS VERSATILE SPACE

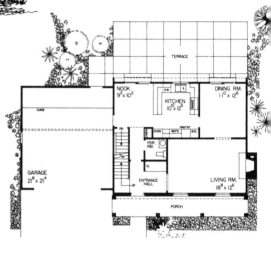

In many two-story homes, there is unused attic space over the garage. This second-story attic conversion is the perfect place for children's sleeping quarters and a play area away from formal living spaces. Alternatively, the plan is an excellent solution for the growing need for in-home offices.

Original Floor Plan

PROBLEM:

▲ Lifestyle changes require more space.

▲ The existing space over the garage has insufficient headroom.

▲ Shape of roof requires some expansion to gain maximum floor space.

▲ There is not enough ventilation or light.

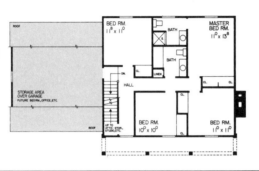

Remodeled Floor Plan

Converting attic space into a usable room is cost-effective and versatile. As a children's space, the room cleverly provides sleeping alcoves and a play area for two children. As a home office, the same space can house a library, a computer alcove and office and conference space.

Home Office

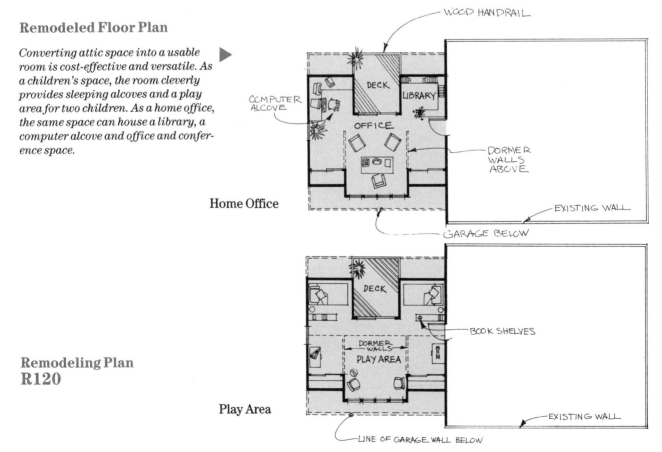

**Remodeling Plan
R120**

Play Area

▲ *View shows attic conversion as office space. Left nook holds computer desk; right nook is library. Deck facing backyard is just outside sliding glass doors.*

ARCHITECT'S VISION

Without help, attics are dark and stuffy places. The conversion provides a window-filled dormer that helps increase floor space, a balcony and an arrangement of spaces that provides flexibility in use.

SOLUTION:

▲ Converting the unused attic to living space is a cost-effective solution to the need for extra space.

▲ The addition of a dormer provides extra head room and vertical space for windows.

▲ A balcony recessed into the attic divides space into useful alcoves and provides ventilation and access to the outdoors.

▲ Low corner alcoves create private nooks for sleeping or computer work.

▲ When the slope of the roof reduces headroom, large closets make perfect use of remaining space.

▲ Windows in the front dormer complement the design of the garage door.

To order construction drawings for this Remodeling Plan, see page 110.

TO ORDER BY PHONE CALL TOLL FREE 1-800-521-6797

▼ *A large dormer complements and balances the garage in the front. In back, the balcony provides a private outdoor space for reading.*

ADDITION SERVES EXERCISE ENTHUSIAST

A second-floor addition to a ranch house can be the least intrusive solution to adding extra space. This addition is geared to the exercise enthusiast. The private enclave includes a changing room and separate bathroom.

PROBLEM:

▲ There is no space for an exercise room.

▲ Exercise equipment is large and needs extra space for use.

▲ A first-floor addition would take up too much of the yard.

▲ The house's single-level curb appeal needs to be maintained.

Original Floor Plan

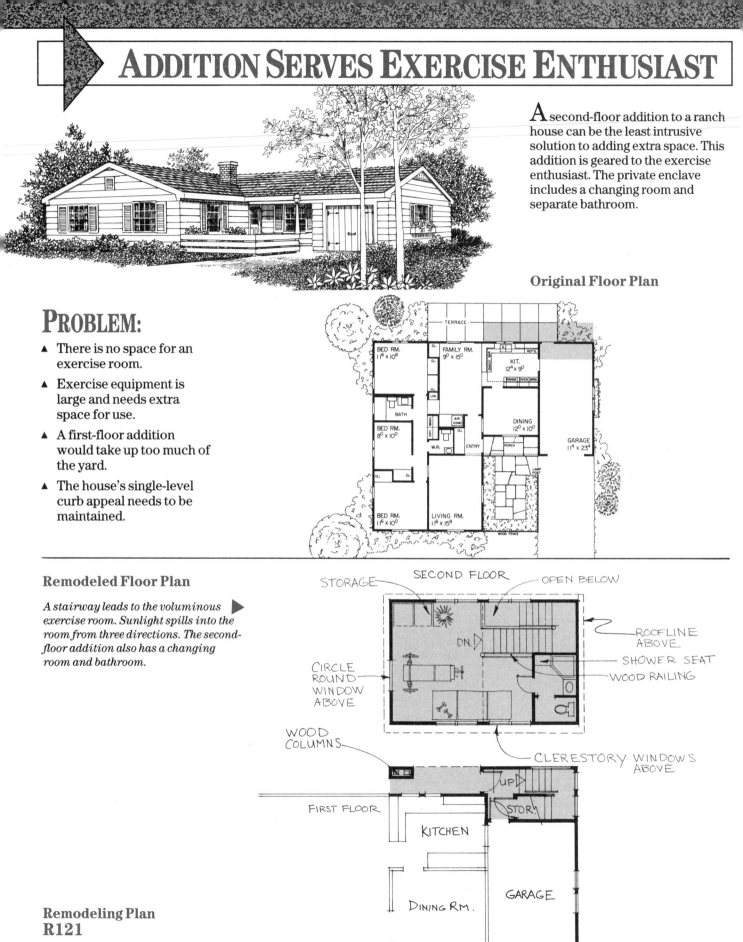

Remodeled Floor Plan

A stairway leads to the voluminous exercise room. Sunlight spills into the room from three directions. The second-floor addition also has a changing room and bathroom. ▶

**Remodeling Plan
R121**

ARCHITECT'S VISION

It is important that a second-story addition not overwhelm the horizontal character of the long ranch house. Clerestory windows balance the addition with the front elevation and maintain privacy.

SOLUTION:

▲ Large windows flood the exercise room with light from three directions.

▲ There is plenty of space for exercise equipment and room to use it.

▲ The loft projects from the rear of the house, shielding the existing kitchen window.

▲ The changing room and bathroom give the space great flexibility. If interests change, the space can become an extra bedroom.

▲ Clerestory windows face the street, balancing the addition with the existing house and providing privacy.

To order construction drawings for this Remodeling Plan, see page 110.

TO ORDER BY PHONE CALL TOLL FREE 1-800-521-6797

▲ *This special space helps make exercise fun. High ceilings allow plenty of space for exercise equipment. Large windows flood the room with light.*

▼ *Clerestory windows call attention to the addition from the street. Major emphasis is on the backyard elevation with its large windows and interesting stairway.*

OUTDOOR KITCHEN IS SUMMER RETREAT

In the days before regular fire protection and air-conditioning, kitchens were in separate buildings near the house. An outdoor kitchen is a boon to summertime cooking and for families who like to barbecue. The kitchen is part of a sheltered outdoor eating center.

Original Floor Plan

PROBLEM:

▲ Outdoor cooking is a balancing act at the barbecue.

▲ Cooking indoors in hot weather can make the whole house hot.

▲ Backyards are not used to full potential.

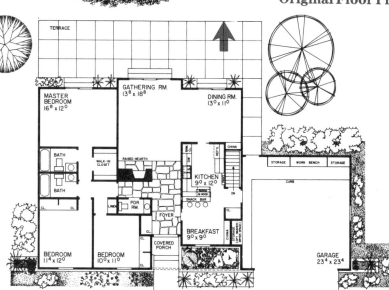

Remodeled Floor Plan

It will be hard to leave this outdoor center with its large deck, covered indoor cooking area complete with stove and refrigerator, and brick barbecue that looks like a fireplace.

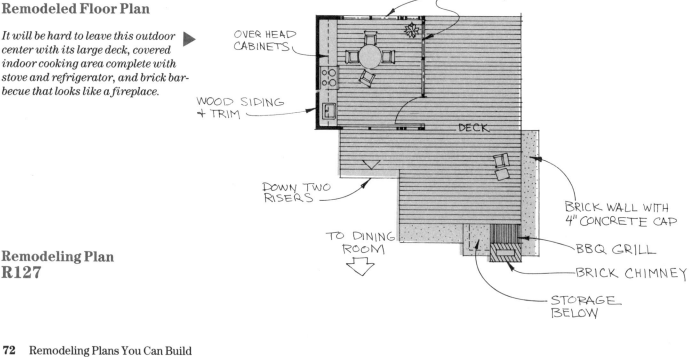

**Remodeling Plan
R127**

ARCHITECT'S VISION

An outdoor kitchen should not look like a tool shed. By integrating the sheltered cooking area with a comfortable deck, benches and a brick barbecue, the whole area becomes as inviting and enchanting as a gazebo.

SOLUTION:

▲ Counter space on either side of the outdoor barbecue gives the chef plenty of preparation room. A cabinet stores barbecue equipment.

▲ The kitchen has a sink, refrigerator and range — all under roof.

▲ The roof rafters that face the deck have translucent panels that keep the kitchen bright.

▲ In areas where insects are a problem, the covered kitchen can be screened in.

▲ The chimney of the brick barbecue balances the shape of the kitchen and carries smoke away from the chef.

▲ Benches provide space for lounging; the deck is big enough for a dining table.

▲ *Mini-kitchen features sink, stove, under-counter refrigerator and plenty of storage—everything needed to prepare meals outdoors. Barbecue area has counter space and additional storage.*

▼ *The covered outdoor kitchen, complete with benches, brick barbecue grill and spacious deck with ample room for patio furniture, truly makes the backyard into an inviting outdoor room.*

To order construction drawings for this Remodeling Plan, see page 110.

TO ORDER BY PHONE CALL TOLL FREE 1-800-521-6797

KIDS' KOTTAGE GIVES PRIVATE REFUGE

P arents of pre-teenagers will appreciate this "kids kottage." The retreat offers parents a place to send the kids to play music and watch television. A teen retreat may be fun for the kids, but it is parents who will benefit most from this addition!

Original Floor Plan

PROBLEM:

▲ Pre-teens and teens like to hang out.

▲ Teens are loud.

▲ Teen and parental agendas often clash.

▲ Parents need to be able to supervise teen activity.

Remodeled Floor Plan

The door of this "kids kottage" opens on a brightly painted graffiti wall. Behind the wall a built-in seating area faces the television (which hides behind the graffiti wall). The design also calls for a special Nintendo center.

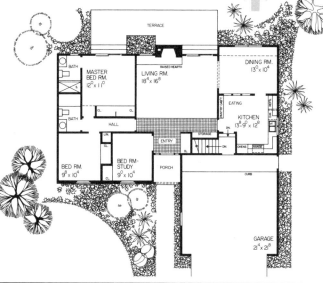

WINDOWS ABOVE AT DIFFERENT LEVELS

RAISED CARPETED PLATFORM

WINDOW SEAT

VAULTED CEILING

CLOSET

CONCRETE PATIO

FURNACE

FRENCH DOOR

Remodeling Plan R126

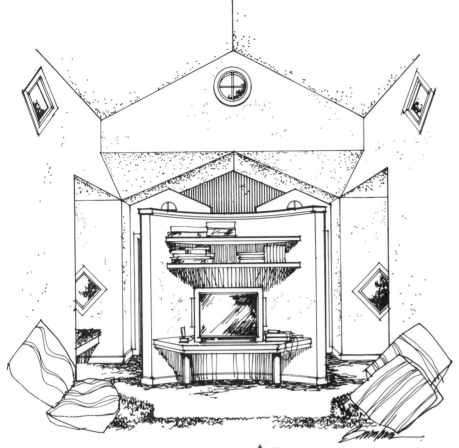

▲ *Kids can break out the popcorn and lounge on the carpeted platform to watch television. Left is study area and right has window seat.*

▼ *Playful shapes, turned windows and a colorful exterior mark this as a place for kids. The rear elevation makes a face with eyes, nose, mouth and even eyebrows.*

ARCHITECT'S VISION

A *special backyard building for kids should blend with a variety of house styles yet be playful and different. Color, a variety of shapes and variations of pattern give the building a sense of exuberance. The graffiti wall, in particular, invites the kids to decorate.*

SOLUTION:

▲ Teens will feel great independence in their own private quarters.

▲ Parents will know where their kids are and what they are doing — but not have to be in the middle of it.

▲ A variety of roof shapes, angled siding and windows suggest the random look of a kid-built play house.

▲ The rear elevation is a house as kids draw it: eyes, nose and mouth.

▲ Screened by a playful graffiti wall, the television is on a counter deep enough for Nintendo playing.

▲ Vaulted ceilings provide space to hang planes and mobiles.

To order construction drawings for this Remodeling Plan, see page 110.

TO ORDER BY PHONE CALL TOLL FREE 1-800-521-6797

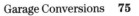

STUDIO MEETS A VARIETY OF NEEDS

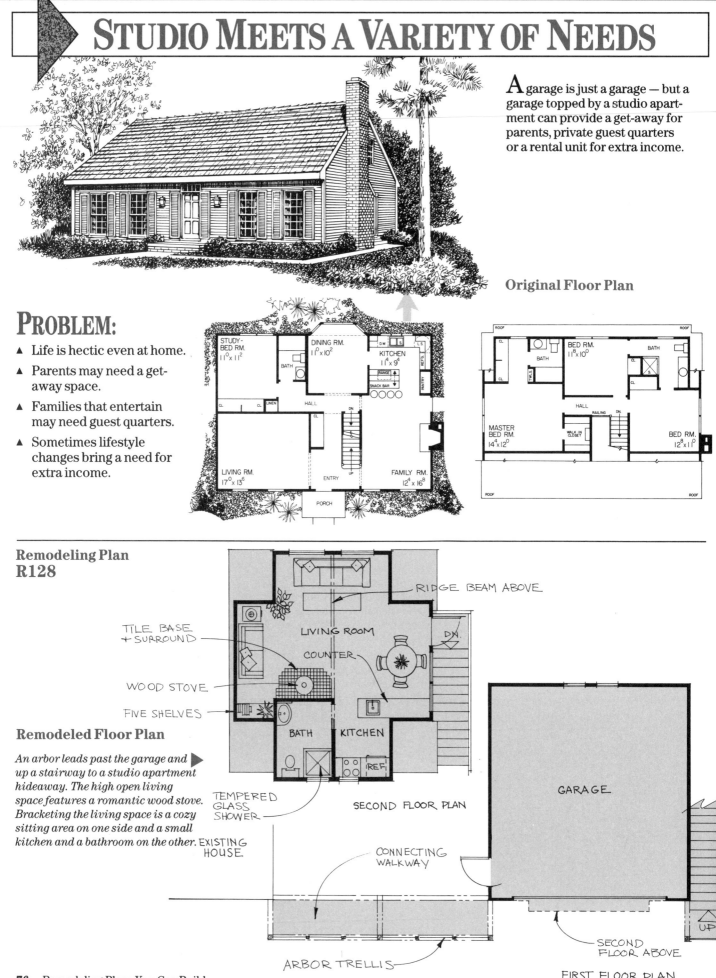

A garage is just a garage — but a garage topped by a studio apartment can provide a get-away for parents, private guest quarters or a rental unit for extra income.

Original Floor Plan

PROBLEM:

▲ Life is hectic even at home.

▲ Parents may need a get-away space.

▲ Families that entertain may need guest quarters.

▲ Sometimes lifestyle changes bring a need for extra income.

STUDY-BED RM. $11^0 \times 11^2$

DINING RM. $11^0 \times 10^2$

KITCHEN $11^4 \times 9^4$

BATH

RANGE

SNACK BAR

PANTRY

REF.S

DW S LS

CL CL LINEN

HALL

CL

DN

LIVING RM. $17^0 \times 13^6$

ENTRY

UP

FAMILY RM. $12^4 \times 16^8$

PORCH

ROOF ROOF

CL

BED RM. $11^8 \times 10^0$

BATH

BATH

CL

CL

HALL

RAILING

DN

MASTER BED RM. $14^4 \times 12^0$

WALK-IN CLOSET

BED RM. $12^8 \times 11^0$

ROOF ROOF

Remodeling Plan R128

RIDGE BEAM ABOVE

TILE BASE + SURROUND

LIVING ROOM

COUNTER

DN.

WOOD STOVE

FIVE SHELVES

BATH

KITCHEN

REF

Remodeled Floor Plan

An arbor leads past the garage and ▶ up a stairway to a studio apartment hideaway. The high open living space features a romantic wood stove. Bracketing the living space is a cozy sitting area on one side and a small kitchen and a bathroom on the other.

TEMPERED GLASS SHOWER

EXISTING HOUSE

SECOND FLOOR PLAN

GARAGE

CONNECTING WALKWAY

SECOND FLOOR ABOVE

UP

ARBOR TRELLIS

FIRST FLOOR PLAN

▲*View from the sitting nook looks toward wood stove and mini-kitchen. Note the ample storage area next to sink and bookshelves next to wood stove.*

ARCHITECT'S VISION

*O*utbuildings visually re-create the sprawling estate. Estates had carriage houses, caretaker cottages, gardener cottages and greenhouses that often interconnected. Today such building can expand the family home, recreate the appeal of another era, and add to the style of the main house.

SOLUTION:

- ▲ An arbor connects the studio/garage with the main house giving the sense of an outbuilding on an estate.

- ▲ The roof shape is a classical mix of gables and dormers that matches many traditional house styles.

- ▲ Inside, the studio feels like the classic artist's hideaway. The vaulted ceiling defines the living space.

- ▲ A small kitchen and bathroom make the space a real apartment rather than a room.

- ▲ A sitting alcove nestled in the gable end is a quiet spot to read.

To order construction drawings for this Remodeling Plan, see page 110.

TO ORDER BY PHONE CALL TOLL FREE 1-800-521-6797

▼ *At the end of a trellised arbor is the studio/garage. Like the carriage houses of old, there is storage for vehicles on the ground level and snug living quarters on the second level. A box bay projecting over the garage door adds interest to the front elevation.*

COTTAGE PROVIDES ULTIMATE HOME GYM

Most homes, even today, seldom have areas set aside for exercise. Fitness equipment is large and takes up even more space in use. This exercise cottage includes room for the exercise equipment as well as a sauna, bathroom, dressing area and spa.

PROBLEM:

▲ Houses aren't designed to accommodate serious exercise enthusiasts.

▲ Exercise equipment is large.

▲ Equipment needs space around it in order to be used.

▲ Gym areas where people are active have different heating and cooling needs than houses.

Original Floor Plan

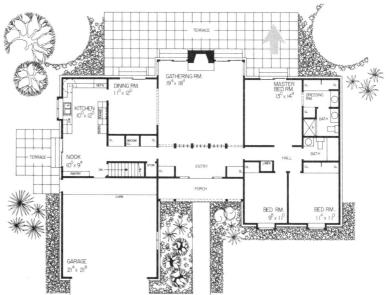

TERRACE

GATHERING RM.
19⁴ x 18⁴

DINING RM.
11⁰ x 12⁰

MASTER BED RM.
13⁰ x 14⁴

DRESSING RM.

BATH

KITCHEN
10⁰ x 12⁰

REFR.

BROOM CL.

BATH

HALL

TERRACE

NOOK
10⁰ x 9⁴

LINEN

PANTRY

DN.

STOR.

ENTRY

CL.

BED RM.
9⁸ x 11⁰

BED RM.
11⁴ x 11⁰

CURB

PORCH

GARAGE
21⁴ x 21⁸

Remodeled Floor Plan

Just outside the existing home's master bedroom, the ultimate personal gym awaits. Closest to the house is the hot tub, bracketed by trellises. The exercise cottage has more than 250 square feet of exercise space, sauna, bathroom and dressing area.

Remodeling Plan
R129

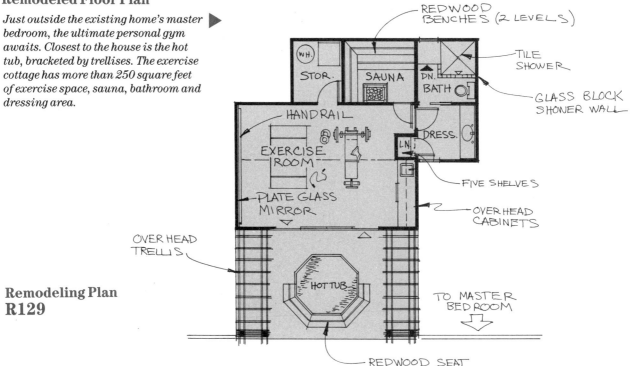

REDWOOD BENCHES (2 LEVELS)

TILE SHOWER

GLASS BLOCK SHOWER WALL

W.H.

STOR.

SAUNA

DN.

BATH

HANDRAIL

EXERCISE ROOM

DRESS.

LN.

FIVE SHELVES

PLATE GLASS MIRROR

OVERHEAD CABINETS

OVERHEAD TRELLIS

HOT TUB

TO MASTER BEDROOM

REDWOOD SEAT

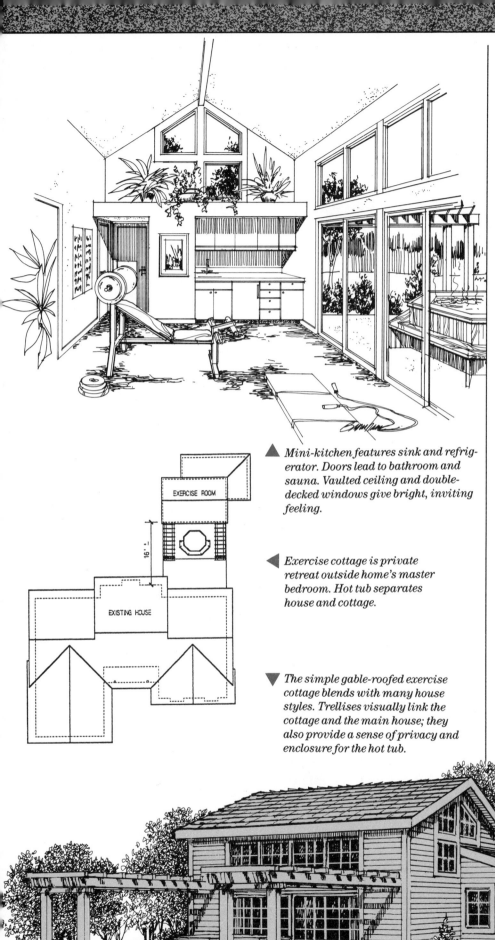

ARCHITECT'S VISION

*E*xercise should be enjoyable and so should the exercise space. A tier of windows above sliding doors floods the room with light. Windows in the exercise cottage face the house to remind owners that the equipment is waiting and to screen exercisers from the neighbors' view.

SOLUTION:

▲ A separate building, the exercise cottage has all of the space and features needed for the perfect workout.

▲ Trellises visually link the exercise cottage and the house and give the spa a comfortable sense of enclosure.

▲ A hot tub, surrounded on three of its six sides with a redwood bench, sits comfortably between the house and the exercise cottage.

▲ The main exercise room provides more than 250 square feet of floor space and more than 12 feet of head room to house the most serious equipment.

▲ Mirrors and a ballet bar line one wall.

▲ The opposite wall has a mini-kitchen, just right for serving sports drinks and juice.

▲ The plan features a sauna, a dressing area with lavatory and linen storage, and a bathroom with a glass-block-walled shower.

Mini-kitchen features sink and refrigerator. Doors lead to bathroom and sauna. Vaulted ceiling and double-decked windows give bright, inviting feeling.

EXERCISE ROOM

16'±

EXISTING HOUSE

Exercise cottage is private retreat outside home's master bedroom. Hot tub separates house and cottage.

The simple gable-roofed exercise cottage blends with many house styles. Trellises visually link the cottage and the main house; they also provide a sense of privacy and enclosure for the hot tub.

To order construction drawings for this Remodeling Plan, see page 110.

TO ORDER BY PHONE CALL TOLL FREE 1-800-521-6797

GARAGE TRANSFORMS INTO GUEST HOUSE

Many families need to help aging parents or children. Transforming a garage into an apartment-like cottage gives these families needed extra space as well as privacy and dignity.

PROBLEM

▲ Extended family members need privacy.

▲ Small space must meet total living needs.

▲ Remodeled garage needs to look "homey."

Original Floor Plan

WORK BENCH - STOR. AREA

TWO CAR GARAGE
$21^5 \times 23^3$

Remodeled Floor Plan

Every square foot of this 528-square-foot garage has been recast as living space. The front door opens on the living room. There is ample dining and kitchen space, too. The bathroom and bedroom are at the back of the former garage.

**Remodeling Plan
R130**

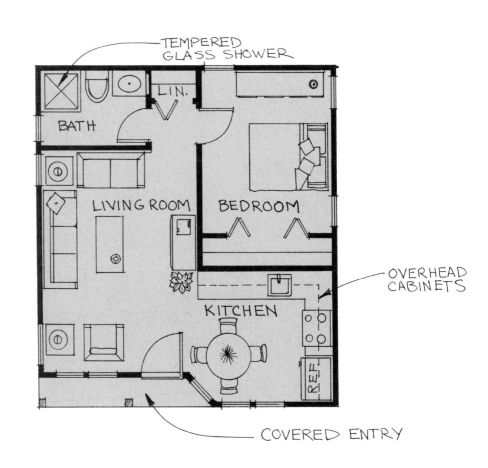

TEMPERED GLASS SHOWER

LIN.

BATH

LIVING ROOM

BEDROOM

KITCHEN

OVERHEAD CABINETS

REF.

COVERED ENTRY

Inside, guest house has all of the elements of home. To left of entry is a dining nook and a full kitchen with generous storage.

ARCHITECT'S VISION

*M*any families want to bring parents or children back into the nest. The best way to preserve the dignity and privacy of relatives who have "lived on their own" is to provide apartment-like space. However, the space should have cottage charm.

SOLUTION

▲ Recessing corner entry by two feet defines entry space; viewing space on diagonal gives it larger appearance.

▲ Generous use of windows brings ample light to living space.

▲ Kitchen has adequate counter space, a dishwasher and full-size oven/range.

▲ Storage gives family members space to keep a lifetime of memories.

▲ Detailing turns utilitarian garage into an inviting cottage.

To order construction drawings for this Remodeling Plan, see page 110.

TO ORDER BY PHONE CALL TOLL FREE 1-800-521-6797

◀ *Guest house demonstrates efficient use of space. Living area has plenty of room for couch, chair, coffee table and television.*

▼ *Recessing entry into corner and generous use of windows takes away the feeling that this was a garage. Placing the entry in the corner gives the interior diagonal views which make it appear larger that it really is.*

THREE FACES CHANGE TWO-STORY APPEAL

This two-story home has a functional floor plan, but needs a face-lift. These homes, often built in mass in subdivisions, all look alike. Curb appeal can make the difference between whether people consider a home appealing or not. Three design solutions offer alternative looks.

Original Floor Plan

PROBLEM:

▲ House has a plain facade with little detailing.

▲ Entry is not inviting.

▲ Porch has awkward unbalanced scale and skimpy posts.

▲ Garage is prominent in overall facade.

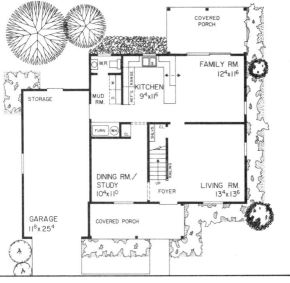

Remodeling Plan
R122

A

▲ *A wrap-around porch with columns, a railing, projecting box bays and an elliptical window on the second floor make an ordinary two-story home feel like a charming farmhouse. Note how porch minimizes prominence of the garage. Box bays on second floor provide window seats inside bedrooms.*

B

▲ *Brick veneer up to the first-floor windows provides a firm base for this facelift. Matched detailing over the covered entry portico and the garage provides*

balance. Shutters proportioned to actually cover the existing windows (if closed) add charm.

ARCHITECT'S VISION

In the 60s and 70s many homes lacked the detailing that makes older traditional homes so appealing. Updating facades can differentiate look-alike homes in a subdivision and add curb appeal. The three options for the two-story home shown all add different kinds of traditional details.

SOLUTION:

▲ Detailing adds charm to an ordinary two-story home.

▲ Porches and porticoes give the home's entry the attention it deserves.

▲ Covered entries provide weather protection for visitors.

▲ Porches on two design solutions minimize prominence of garage.

▲ On third solution, the repeat of the same detailing on garage and entry portico provide an inviting rhythm and balance.

C

▲ *The third solution unifies the porch and garage as one mass — the second-story above the porch as a second mass. The new two-story pop-out to the right is a major vertical element that balances the garage. The eye travels from*

the base of the garage in a diagonal line to the gable on the second story. The overall effect provides protection for the entry and balances the garage with the rest of the house.

To order construction drawings for this Remodeling Plan, see page 110.

TO ORDER BY PHONE CALL TOLL FREE 1-800-521-6797

FACELIFTS REFLECT DIFFERENT AGES

Exterior changes can have dramatic results. The original split-foyer 60s house has little charm. The formal placement of windows does lend itself to formal solutions. Most people would be amazed to find the same floor plan behind the Southern Belle and the Frank Lloyd Wright-inspired facades shown here.

PROBLEM:

- ▲ Two-story home lacks detail.
- ▲ The front entrance is merely another opening in the facade.
- ▲ There is no design element to balance the asymmetrical front door.
- ▲ House has no focal point to draw viewer's eye.

Original Floor Plan

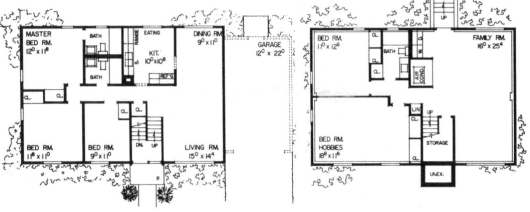

**Remodeling Plan
R123**

A

▲ *Classic materials — stone quoins, brick siding, heavy lintels and large shutters — transform this contemporary home into a Southern Belle. Two-story portico makes the entry the focal point. Fluted columns, arched transom over the front door and railing on the portico give the entry great presence.*

B

▲ *Another solution, emphasizing horizontal lines, provides an equally
dramatic change. Wood shake shingles
on the first floor and wood siding on the
second establish the horizontal pattern.
Box bays add definition and interest to
the first story. Wood banding under*
*and over the first-floor windows and on
top of the bays reinforces the pattern.
The trellised entry rises a story-and-
one-half. A horizontal band of square
windows forms a transom over the
front entry.*

C

▲ *The third facelift is just as dramatic.
Vertical accents at the windows and
gable roofs added to the simple roof line
make the house stand tall. A large*
*dormer over the living room window
adds curb appeal to what started off as
a rather boring house.*

ARCHITECT'S VISION

*T*he same house looks radically
different depending on the
exterior design solution.
Classical materials, careful
proportion and prominent entry
turn the contemporary home
into a Southern plantation.
Differentiating the exterior facing
of the first and second floors
lowers the home's scale in the
Frank Lloyd Wright-inspired
design. Projecting box bays and
a trellised entry also change the
home. Vertical accents and
gables give the contemporary
house a third inviting look.

SOLUTION:

▲ Attention to detail brings very
different changes.

▲ Two solutions include prominent entry porticos to give
prominence to the front door
and to protect visitors from the
weather.

▲ Prominent entry porticos
balance the asymmetrical
design and provide a strong
focal point for the facade.

▲ The Southern Belle design
emphasizes the two-story
height. Stone quoins in the
corner draw the eye upward as
does the railing on the entry
portico.

▲ The Frank Lloyd Wright-inspired
solution emphasizes the horizontal lines of the house. Wood
shakes on the first floor and siding on the second establish the
horizontal pattern.

▲ The third facelift uses classic
dormers to give the house eyebrows that emphasize the vertical rather than the horizontal
nature of the existing home. A
large dormer over the living
room window dramatically
changes the formerly boring
house.

**To order construction
drawings for this Remodeling
Plan, see page 110.**

**TO ORDER BY PHONE
CALL TOLL FREE
1-800-521-6797**

SPLIT-LEVEL TRIES ON NEW LOOKS

Split-level plans represent an unusual challenge. Typically, such houses have a slightly below-grade garage topped by the home's bedrooms. Kitchen, dining and living areas occupy the grade-level floor of the home. To end up with an attractive facelift, the obviously prominent two-story section must balance the single-story section without obscuring the home's entrance.

Original Floor Plan

PROBLEM:

▲ Awkward two-story section is difficult to balance with the less prominent one-story section.

▲ The front entrance in the single-level section is visually hard to find.

▲ Split-level designs have few historical antecedents.

**Remodeling Plan
R124**

A

▲ *Brick on the first-floor level and shingles on the second floor emphasize horizontal lines and balance the two sections of the house. A strong entry portico detailed with columns draws attention to the front door. The line of the second-story gable flows into the gable on the entry portico, which also serves to balance the overall mass of the house.*

B

▲ *Drawing from the massive shingle-style California bungalows of architects Greene and Greene, this design tackles the challenge of proportion and scale. A large bay with a sunburst design adds* *interest to the two-story section. Massive columns balance the design, support the front porch and draw attention to the front door.*

ARCHITECT'S VISION

*T*he front door in the home's first level deserves an important place in the exterior design. The design challenge is to shift visual attention from the massive two-story section of the house to the front entry where it belongs.

SOLUTION:

▲ Emphasis on horizontal lines brings the bulky two-story section into balance with the rest of the house.

▲ The first solution adds a strong front entry portico. The gabled roof of the second story extends to provide one side of the entry portico which balances the two sections of the house.

▲ The second design solution emphasizes the front porch, which helps focus attention on the front door. A projecting box bay on the second story over the garage repeats the column detail of the porch and balances the mass of the two-story section.

▲ Gable accents the large living-room window while a semi-circular dormer calls attention to the entry. Sliding doors from upstairs bedrooms lead to a new balcony over the garage, cleverly de-emphasizing the garage.

To order construction drawings for this Remodeling Plan, see page 110.

**TO ORDER BY PHONE
CALL TOLL FREE
1-800-521-6797**

C

▲ *The balcony over the garage de-emphasizes the importance of the garage and gives bedrooms access to the outdoors. A* *new gable roof emphasizes the living room while a semi-circular dormer draws attention to the entry.*

THREE LOOKS CHANGE RANCH'S FACE

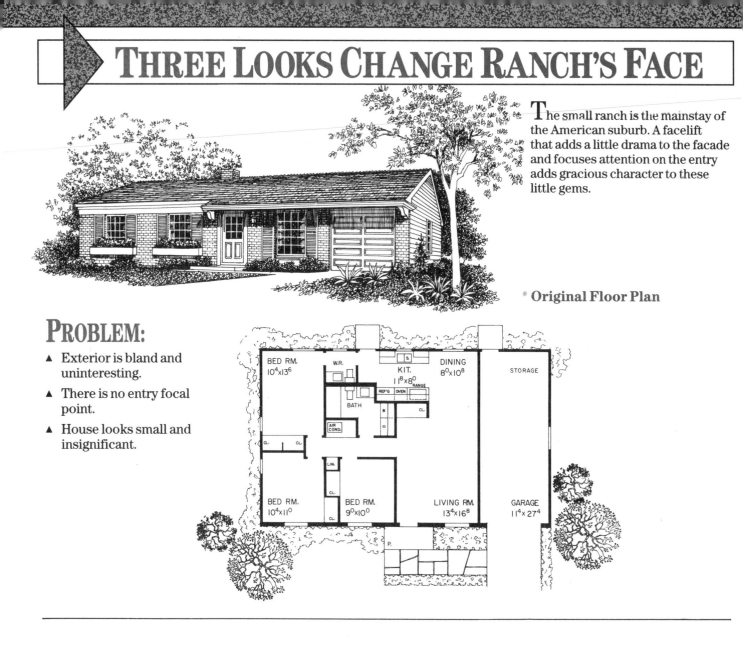

The small ranch is the mainstay of the American suburb. A facelift that adds a little drama to the facade and focuses attention on the entry adds gracious character to these little gems.

Original Floor Plan

PROBLEM:

▲ Exterior is bland and uninteresting.

▲ There is no entry focal point.

▲ House looks small and insignificant.

BED RM. 10⁴x13⁶   W.R.   KIT. 11⁸x8⁰ RANGE   DINING 8⁰x10⁸   STORAGE

S   REF'G   OVEN   CL.   BATH   AIR COND.

CL.   CL.   LIN.   CL.   CL.

BED RM. 10⁴x11⁰   BED RM. 9⁰x10⁰   LIVING RM. 13⁴x16⁸   GARAGE 11⁴x27⁴

P.

Remodeling Plan
R125

A

▲ *Brick veneer on the exterior, coupled with horizontal banding, double-hung windows and a series of projecting gables that includes an entry portico, give this house a prosperous and substantial appearance from the street.*

B

▲ *An oversized gable brings a dramatic change of scale. The upper sash of the new double-hung windows and the garage door windows match, creating a* *rhythm to the facade. Cedar shakes and wood banding give the house the charm of a country cottage.*

ARCHITECT'S VISION

The existing simple gable roof is also the secret to the facelift solutions. Projecting gables provide a sculptural image and focus attention on the entry. The type and position of gables in the following solutions provide very different results.

SOLUTION:

▲ Gables added to the house provide curb appeal.

▲ One solution adds a gabled portico over the entry.

▲ In another solution, the new gable is larger than the original and makes the house seem larger from the street.

▲ The third solution uses a series of arches and gables to make the small ranch look longer. Arches provide some Spanish seasoning to the design.

▲ Changing the size and proportion of windows also gives the house added curb appeal.

C

▲ *Tall windows with arched transoms and gables that project over the garage and the entry portico add presence and* *a bit of Spanish seasoning to the new brick facade.*

To order construction drawings for this Remodeling Plan, see page 110.

TO ORDER BY PHONE CALL TOLL FREE 1-800-521-6797

HOW TO ADAPT OUR PLANS TO FIT YOUR HOME

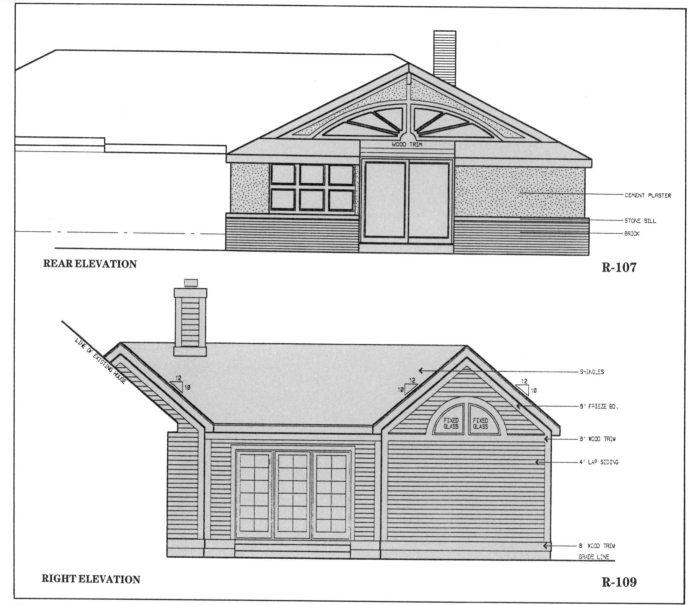

REAR ELEVATION

WOOD TRIM

CEMENT PLASTER

STONE SILL

BRICK

R-107

LINE OF EXISTING HOUSE

FIXED GLASS   FIXED GLASS

SHINGLES

8" FRIEZE BD.

8" WOOD TRIM

4" LAP SIDING

8" WOOD TRIM

GRADE LINE

RIGHT ELEVATION

R-109

Master suites offer wonderful retreats for parents of teenage children. Plan R-107 (above and page 54) expands a ranch house. First-floor master suites (bottom, Plan R-109, page 58) adapt one and one-half and two-story family houses to the single-floor living empty nesters prefer.

Now you have looked over our plans. Perhaps one is just perfect for you and will attach to your home with very little modification. If your home is a mirror image of the plan as shown, you can order plans reversed to attach to your home. However, your home may be different from the existing home pictured. How do you adapt our plans to fit more precisely?

MATCHING YOUR LIFESTYLE TO YOUR PLAN

The first thing to consider is the flow of your existing floor plan.

Is your home one or two stories? On a one-story home, care must be taken to not overwhelm the original house with an addition. The concern with a two-story home is to not obscure second-story windows with

the addition. In both cases, the proposed addition's proportion becomes a question of balance. If one of our plans is just right, you can work with Home Planners or your builder/remodeler to customize the plan in order to bring it into scale with your home. (See page 110 for more details on our exclusive Home Remodeler Service.)

Is the floor plan really like yours? Your house might not be a Colonial, but might have the center entry with the living room on one side and the kitchen and dining room on the other, as is typical of Colonials. A key issue for any addition is the connection between the existing house and the new space. Will you be able to connect the addition to a room or hallway with the same use as shown in the existing house plan in this book?

A number of these plans work very well for styles other than the house with which they are shown. Ask yourself — is my bedroom in a back corner? Is my kitchen at the back of the house? Does my hallway work in a way similar to the plan the addition is shown attached to?

Are your bedrooms on the first floor or the second? Even if all of your bedrooms are on the second floor, you could add a first-floor master suite. Such suites convert a family home into an empty-nesters' retreat. For example, plan R-107 shown on pages 54 and 55 and plan R-109 on pages 58 and 59 could be customized as first-floor master suites for two-story homes.

If your kitchen is in the front of the house, you have more of a challenge than one in the rear because an addition to the front elevation often changes the character of the house. Front- facing additions also run into potential problems with meeting local zoning requirements and set-backs. However, if the existing house is on a large lot, some of our kitchen plans can be adapted for a front- or side-yard addition. Such plans would need to be carefully detailed and adapted to balance with the existing house and maintain its overall character.

Plan R-101 on pages 30 and 31 and R-103 on pages 34 and 35 are two kitchen additions that easily adapt to an appropriate scale and attach to a variety of house styles with rear-facing kitchens.

Master bedrooms in a rear corner with a small bathroom (or sometimes no bathroom at all) are ripe for many of our master-suite remodeling plans. Usually the backyard has the most room for an addition. Bumping out the back corner of the house frequently creates a private sheltered garden area perfect for your patio or deck.

You need to ask yourself some questions if you want to consider a

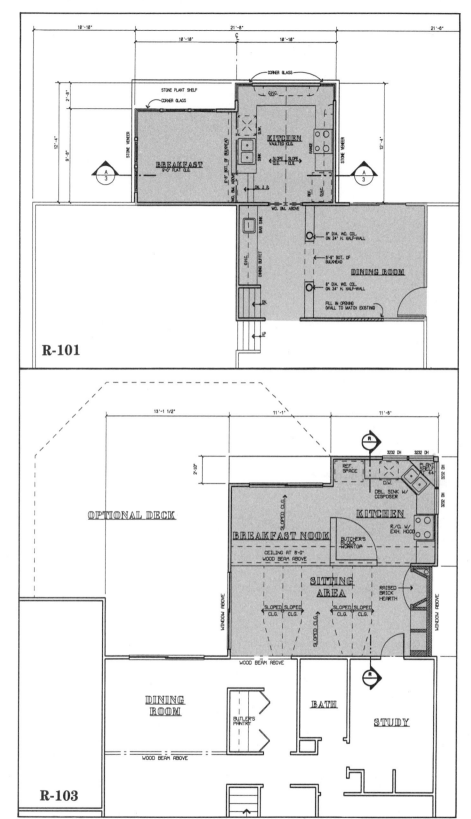

Plan R-101 (page 30) and R-103 (page 34) are two kitchen addition plans that can adapt easily to a variety of house styles with rear-facing kitchens. Both plans include informal breakfast areas. Plan 103 features an intriguing sitting area reminiscent of the old keeping room in historic houses.

plan for a different application than shown. Were I to adapt this particular plan to my style house would it help or impair circulation? Would traffic have to pass through seating areas? Carefully compare the room flow of your home to the existing home. Play with the plan to see if it

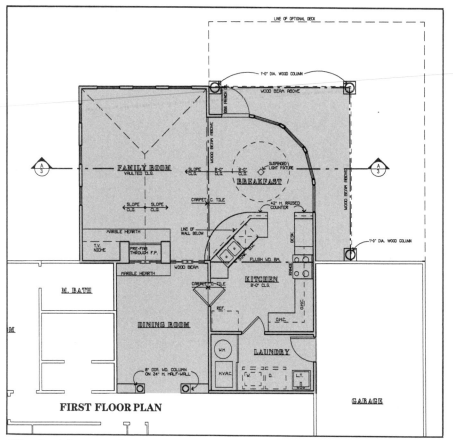

FIRST FLOOR PLAN

What do visitors see when they open the front door? With Plan R-100, above and page 28, the view lines are through the living room past two columns flanking the new dining room and through the two-sided fireplace into the family room. The effect is formal, inviting and doubles the perceived size of the house.

Plan 103, above and page 34, is a classic. The sitting room is a modern interpretation of the keeping room in historic houses. The kitchen opens into this inviting family space.

would also work in a slightly different location or orientation to your home and lot. You may find you have been adapting your lifestyle to fit your house rather than having your home fit your lifestyle.

Think about your lifestyle and use of rooms. What do you or visitors see from the front door? You probably don't want to open the front door and be able to see your kitchen sink. A view from the front door that looks through the house to a back garden is desirable since it makes even a small house seem large and inviting. Needless to say, you certainly don't want to walk through a bedroom to get to your new family-room addition.

How do you want to live? Does the addition satisfy some basic lifestyle needs? How do you live now? If you could re-make your house to satisfy your needs what would you want?

Many families want separate adult-only and family spaces. Family-room additions provide space for informal family fun and leave living rooms as tidy parlors in which to entertain adult friends.

Kitchens have been reborn as the heart of the home, especially when the remodel includes a family room or sitting room with fireplace. Plan 103, shown on pages 34 and 35, is a classic. It features a sitting area reminiscent of the keeping room in many historic houses.

Even cooks who never cook want all the "toys." Luxury homes often have an intimate area scaled for the preparation of everyday meals and another area with a butlers pantry and generous counter space for catering parties. Your kitchen re-make can add a touch of luxury to even the dullest home.

Two work triangles are quite common so that two or more can cook at once. Kitchen islands provide space for cooking, cleaning produce or eating. You may need more space for appliances — and more appliances. In homes where the owners entertain a lot, it is not uncommon to have two dishwashers and two ovens.

To make the kitchen easy to work in, the stove should be near a sink and have counter space on either side. The dishwasher should be near the dish storage area to maximize efficient unloading. The microwave is most efficient when placed near the refrigerator, since its primary use is heating frozen foods and leftovers.

Our master bedroom plans offer you a golden opportunity to create a personal retreat. In new homes, master bedrooms have quiet sitting areas. They frequently have fireplaces — some of them feature a raised hearth and may be two-sided separating the bathing area from the sleeping area but visible from both. Dual vanities, separate showers and toilet compartments are also common. Less common but available are sauna units and units to convert the shower into a steam room. Walk-in closets and dressing areas are also important parts of the contemporary master suite.

Do these master suite features meet your needs? Do you want a garden, a pool or a spa just outside your bedroom door? Do you need an exercise area?

Do you need an area for special activities, an apartment for relatives, an exercise area, a teen retreat or a home office? These plans answer many of your lifestyle needs and can be adapted to your existing home.

Home is a refuge, a safe haven for many families. Just as a make-over rejuvenates a person, a make-over for your home can rejuvenate your feelings and comfort about being at home. A facelift for the front of your home can take years off its appearance. It will not only give you an emotional lift but will also contribute to resale value by improving your home's all-important "curb appeal."

Consider the aesthetics and style of your home and whether the changes and additions you want to make will harmonize. A Colonial home with a contemporary addition will look architecturally impaired. It is perfectly OK to change the entire spirit of your home, but use common sense. Just look at the dramatic changes achieved by the facelifts for plan R-123 on pages 84 and 85. Remember that the most important consideration is that both the new and old must look like they belong together and belong to you.

ADAPTING THE PLAN TO YOUR HOME

You have found the Home Planners remodeling plan that meets your needs and enhances your lifestyle. Now what? Even if your home is nearly identical to the existing house shown with your remodeling plan, some modifications and adaptations will need to be made.

Not all homes are on level ground or look alike even if they have the same plan. There are a number of considerations in adapting your new remodeling plan to your existing home.

The first consideration is the site. Does it slope? How is the drainage? What is the soil like? Are there unstable soil conditions? Where are the utility easements?

A sloping site can actually provide an opportunity for a walk-out space below the addition. Additions can be built on piers and cantilevered over a hilly site. You can improve drainage by re-routing water away from the addition. Some soils may require special foundations. A

soils engineer is the proper expert to evaluate site conditions. Easements should have been marked on the survey made when you purchased your home. Double-check with the local utilities — sometimes surveys are incorrect — or have a new one done.

Look at your floor plan and our remodeling plan. Many of the remodeling plans attach to the existing house through a hallway or kitchen. An existing bedroom is often the connecting point for master-suite additions. You wouldn't want to walk through your bedroom to get to your new family room. Typically, you wouldn't want to walk through the kitchen to get to your new master suite. Home Planners or a local builder/remodeler or architect can adapt the plan you like to your own existing floor plan. (See page 110 for information on our exclusive Home Remodeler Service).

Roofs come in gable, hip, flat, mansard, gambrel and a variety of other shapes. You don't want your

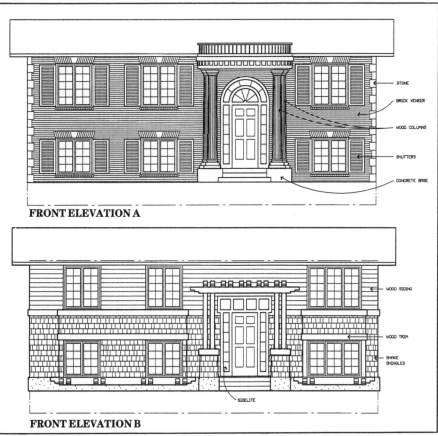

FRONT ELEVATION A

FRONT ELEVATION B

It is hard to believe that the two facelifts shown above (Plan R-123, page 84) started with the same basic two-story house. The high entry portico of the Southern Bell version emphasizes the home's height. The Frank Lloyd Wright-inspired version emphasizes horizontal lines.

Exterior style is another important consideration. Your addition should blend with your existing house. Clockwise from top: A — Long, low, Contemporary Ranch with wood siding; B — Pueblo Style with stucco, soft sculpted shapes and exposed rafter ends; D — Traditional with dormers, clapboard siding and shutters; C — Contemporary Mediterranean with clay-tile roof and stucco siding.

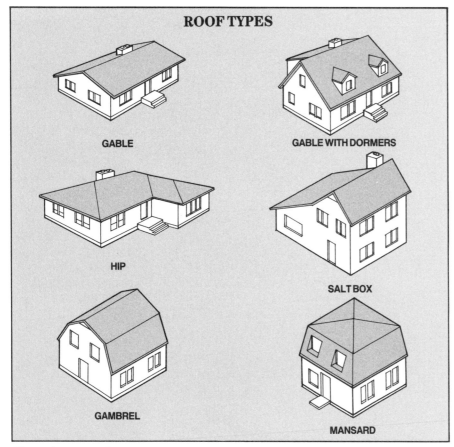

ROOF TYPES

GABLE

GABLE WITH DORMERS

HIP

SALT BOX

GAMBREL

MANSARD

The roof on your addition should imitate or complement the one on your existing house. Roofs come in a variety of shapes: gable, salt box, gambrel, hip and mansard. There are also partial roof shapes: shed dormers and single, gable-roofed dormers.

new addition to look like it dropped into place without regard for what was already there. Your new space must integrate with the old. Care must be taken to extend, complement or carefully contrast with your existing roof lines. Alternatively, you can give an exterior facelift to a totally out-dated house in order to match the new style introduced by a room addition.

Is your house brick or frame, one- or two-stories high? The style, materials and composition of the existing structure will make a difference in the way you connect new and old.

Is your existing home clad in clapboard, vertical cedar planks or shingles? Is it brick, block or stone? Or is it stucco? Is the style the Monterey, Mission or Pueblo styles of the West or Southwest? Or is it the Colonial, Cape Cod or Cottage styles of the South and East? Is the house an historic Italianate or Queen Anne style?

You don't need to mimic your existing house, but you do need to complement its style. Sometimes a band of brick below the window line will coordinate a clapboard-

If your site is hilly, you have several options in placement of an addition. In the contemporary house shown above, the front elevation is at grade level at the top of the hill. The lower level, near the base of the slope, has a walk-out basement. Space on the side of the house could be the place to add on.

sided addition with an all-brick existing house. You need to be aware of the elements of style that will help coordinate new and old. Consider using a trellis or patio to form a transitional link that ties new and old together.

Details make all the difference in the world. Does your existing home have shutters and window boxes? Put shutters and window boxes on the addition. Are there brackets under the eaves or windows? Put brackets under the eaves or windows in your addition. Matching details is the best way to achieve a seamless remodel.

SCOPING OUT YOUR SITE

Verify set-back requirements, utility easements, zoning regulations and restrictions on size or height first. If your plans encroach on any of these requirements, you'll need to go before the zoning board to get a variance. Don't panic and don't ignore code restrictions. As irritating as they may seem, they are there for the community's harmony and protection. Follow procedures carefully, since getting permission to add-on is the cornerstone of a successful remodeling project.

The addition plans shown are designed for relatively flat, suburban sites. The one you choose can be adapted to your specific site either by Home Planners or through a local builder/remodeler. (See page 110 for more details on our exclusive customizing service.)

If your site is hilly, there are several options. You can build a walk-out basement foundation and gain extra space. If the site is very steep, with a sharp drop-off, you can build the addition on piers cantilevered over the site. If your house is nestled into a hill, you can usually re-contour and drain the necessary area. The addition can also step up with the grade of the site or follow the site contour and be placed at the side of the house.

Irregular grades require reshaping and draining away from the house and addition. Often such contouring is needed to protect the existing house, or to overcome existing drainage problems.

A soils engineer can advise you on how to treat difficult-site situations. Sometimes the answer will be to post-tension the slab, a method

of reinforcing the foundation. Other times you will need to sink caissons deep enough to reach stable soil. Don't try to cheat on the foundation. If problems develop later, it will be far more costly to fix them and it could affect the resale value of your home.

Mature landscaping can add considerable value to your home. Study the vegetation around the area of your proposed addition. Some trees, shrubs and other plants can be moved, protected during remodeling and returned to an area near the original location. Since such transplanting is not always successful, consider that option carefully.

Think about adjusting the shape or placement of your addition to save mature trees. Experts say each mature tree adds as much as $1000 to the value of a property. Since trees take many years to reach maturity, it makes sense to preserve your existing trees.

You will also want to protect nearby trees during construction. Heavy construction equipment compresses the soil and smothers tree roots. Alter the construction methods or hand-dig founda-

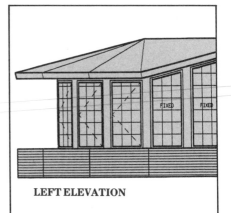

LEFT ELEVATION

Deep overhangs balanced by a planter protect windows from excessive heat gain. Plan is R-115 also shown on page 46.

tions around valuable landscape specimens.

If you plan to add gravel paths or driveways, be careful of the type of gravel. Limestone will kill oak trees. In such cases you would be wise to consult a professional landscaper before starting your addition.

Call your local utilities to determine placement of underground utility feeds and location of easements. Utility feeds can be moved, though if you retie into sewers or water mains, for example, it will add substantially to the cost of remodeling.

Orientation of house and site is another important factor. If the placement of your addition exposes many windows to the Western sun, you can add roof overhangs, build a high garden wall or plant deciduous trees to protect the addition from excessive heat gain. You can also reduce the number of West-facing windows and compensate for the lost light by adding windows on the East side or skylights.

In harsh winter climates, you might move a North-facing patio door to the East.

In Southern or Western climates, roof overhangs can be made deeper or provisions made to add awnings to protect windows and avoid solar heat gain.

Some addition plans can be easily flipped, creating a mirror image of the original, in order to be properly oriented to a site. If you decide to reverse a plan, double-check that it

still flows correctly in relationship to the existing plan of your home.

MARRYING THE FLOOR PLAN

Each home has a distinctive floor plan. Even homes built in subdivisions will have had adjustments made during construction or adaptations made that render them unique. Compare the plan of your home to the plan shown on the page with the addition you like — check similarities and differences between existing plans.

Many additions connect through a hall or a room space. Check to see that the addition can be similarly connected to your home. It's fine to add a master bedroom on to an existing bedroom that becomes a sitting room. It would not be fine to walk through your bedroom to get to the new family room.

Similarly, linking new kitchens with existing kitchens and linking new family rooms through existing kitchens are usually good circulation solutions. You probably do not want to enter your new master suite by walking through the kitchen. If

you're not sure, ask a local realtor for advice. You do not want to penalize yourself at resale for doing something so unusual that it meets no one else's lifestyle needs.

If a couple of feet added or subtracted here or there from the addition would make it work for you, consult a professional to make sure the addition plan continues to flow. You may need structural adaptations to make plan changes.

Room additions can attach to any style house. If you like a plan and it would attach well to your home, you will need only to adapt the exterior design to coordinate with the style of your home. Often this change can be done with details such as shutters or brackets over eaves. An alternative is to modify the existing house to match the style of the addition. This can often be done with such "cosmetic" changes as shutters, siding, brickrows, eave decoration or other add-on details.

Whatever you decide, it is crucial that the new and the old meld together. The best additions look as if

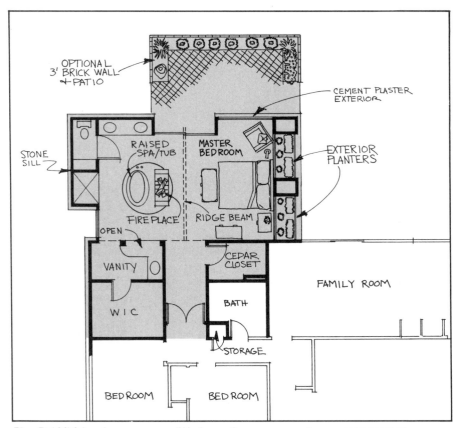

Plan R-107 (also shown on page 54) shows the proper way to connect a master suite addition to a home. Connection through a hallway or existing bedroom works; connection through the family room is usually an awkward solution.

nothing has been added on because old and new blend together well.

TAKING IT TO THE TOP

Crucial to the success of any addition is its attachment at the roof line. Roof attachment can dramatically enhance overall appearance. A poor attachment can lead to structural problems, primarily through leaks.

Typically, your existing roof structure will remain, and the new roof will connect to the existing roof. The extra weight of the new roof will not usually be a problem.

One of the most important details is that eave lines and fascia lines match. If the existing roof has deep overhangs, copy them. If the existing roof has projecting brackets, reproduce them.

Sometimes, if the house is too old to find matching details, you will want to replace the older details to match the new. Be careful following this last option. If your home is historic, you'll be better off paying extra for custom-made accents that match your historic detailing.

Roof pitch should be similar but not necessarily identical. The human eye has difficulty detecting slight

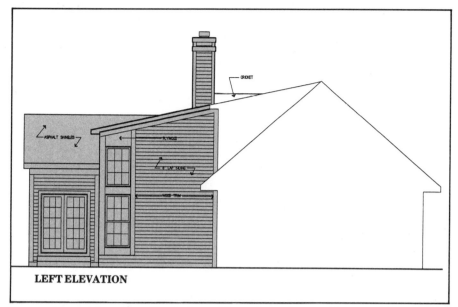

LEFT ELEVATION

You need to match and coordinate the roof lines of your home with your addition. In this example from Plan R-116 (page 48), the roof line of an existing dormer extends to provide a cathedral ceiling in the family room. The kitchen and breakfast areas have gable roofs that match the existing gable on the home.

differences in pitch, but focuses immediately on mis-matched fascias. If you need a 6/12 pitch (one that slopes six inches in 12 inches) to align the fascias of an existing 5/12 roof, few will realize that the pitches are not the same.

A gable-roofed addition that is perpendicular to the existing house is relatively easy to attach. Note how connections are made between a gable end and a gable-roofed house and a hip-roofed house.

There are many roof design lessons contained in our plans. If the addition projects from the end of the house, you can use the slope of the roof to define the gable pitch.

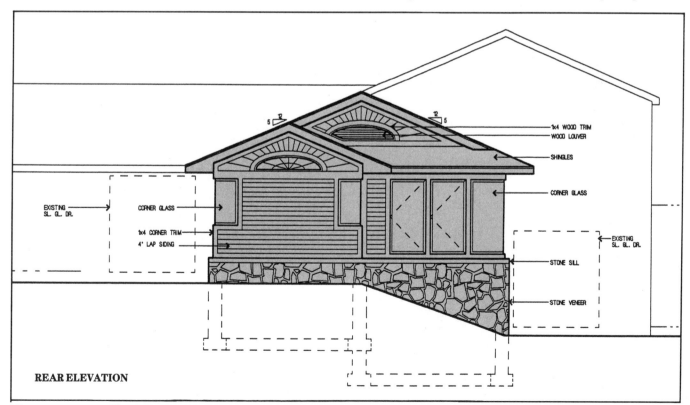

REAR ELEVATION

There are many roof lessons contained in our plans. Plan R-101 (page 30) is an excellent example of how to add gable roofs. The two gables on the addition balance the existing roof of a tri-level and add character that enhances the entire home.

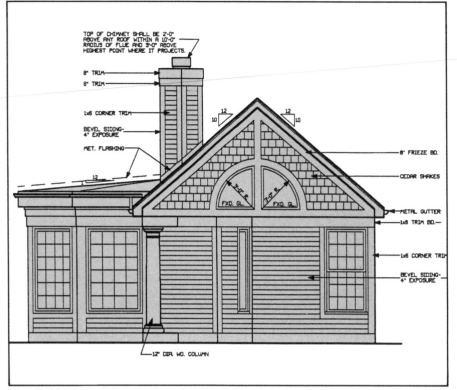

Plan R-114 (page 44) uses a low-pitched, three-sided roof similar to those on bay windows. This low roof over the breakfast area complements the gable. A low-pitched roof can be a good solution for a one-story addition that would otherwise obscure second-story windows on the existing house.

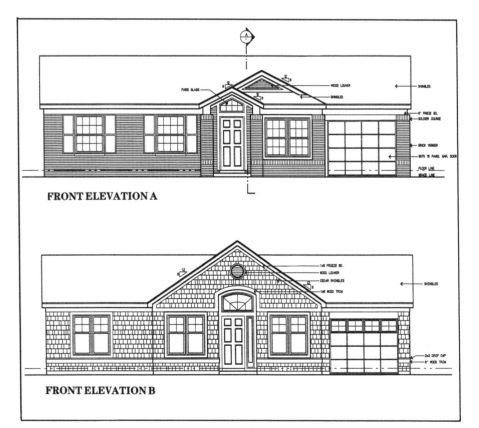

FRONT ELEVATION A

FRONT ELEVATION B

Blend your existing house with the new addition by matching existing siding or changing the siding for the whole house. Above are two elevations from Plan R-125 (page 88), that dramatically alter the front elevation of the same basic ranch home. Notice how much larger the home looks with the addition of the prominent front-facing gable shown in elevation B (bottom).

See plan R-101 on pages 30 and 31 and R-104 on pages 36 and 37 for good examples.

You don't always have to mimic the roof style of the existing house. Plan R-103 on pages 34 and 35 uses a series of dormers to connect an addition to a Cape Cod house's steep gable. Plan R-113 on pages 42 and 43 uses an arched roof as part of the room addition. Plan R-114 on pages 44 and 45 uses a low-pitched, three- sided roof similar to those used on bay windows.

Often, when a new roof ties into an old roof, the urge is to reshingle the whole roof. Check the age and condition of your roof to see if reshingling the whole structure is necessary.

The key is that the whole house should look of a piece. Part of the charm of cottage architecture is the variety of pitches and details used to create a whole. The trick with roofs is to have a consistent vision of unity.

HITTING THE WALL

Each of our remodeling plans, by necessity, makes some assumptions about the structure of the existing house. Depending on the age, style and materials used to build your home, structure can be very different from what we show.

Don't worry. This usually means that you will have to use different techniques than we show to connect your home and the new addition. Most structural differences can be worked around and just need to be studied.

Examine or bring in an expert to examine the structure of your house. Differences between the existing house as shown in this book and your house should be discussed with Home Planners or a local engineer. (See page 110 for information on our exclusive Home Remodeler Service that provides a low-cost way to alter these plans to suit your exact needs.)

KEEPING IT IN STYLE

Existing homes come in a variety of styles and materials. In fact, with our facelift plan R-123 on pages 84 and 85, it is hard to believe that either new design is the same house as the original. Each facade exhibits a complete change in spirit.

Often recasting details and exterior materials will bring about equally dramatic changes. If your home is the "Plain Jane" of the neighborhood, you might want to combine an addition with a facelift. In that case, you'll want to tie the style of the facelift together with the addition.

The whole-house make-over concept is similar to fashion makeovers of people. Dressed for the role, a person can look casual, intelligent, sophisticated, rich or poor. Fashion magazines regularly differentiate between high fashion and the classics, and so it is with houses. You have to decide which style represents and fits into your neighborhood as well as your lifestyle.

With their clothes off, many houses are the same in basic structure and plan. Builders of new houses purposely offer a variety of exterior designs for the same plan to avoid subdivision neighborhoods that look monotonous.

Examine your basic structure. Older houses have often suffered previously from incompatible additions. What was the basic structure? What is worth keeping? What do you need to do to create a unified whole?

Often you can blend the existing with the new either by re-siding the completed structure with the same materials or by re-using some of the existing house's materials as design elements in a new addition.

In older homes, the windows may have deteriorated. New windows, properly installed, reduce air-infiltration, one of the biggest energy-wasters. New windows use sealed layered glass, tints, films and inert gases to increase energy efficiency. You might want to replace the windows in your existing house and match them to new windows in the addition. This is another way to link old and new and, as an added bonus, save energy.

To match the house in scale, you can enlarge or decrease the size of the addition — both in height and square footage. You must take care that all of the elements such as the roof planes continue to balance proportionally with the entire house.

Often the trick to integrating the old and new is to match the details. Shown above are two elevations of Plan R-117 (page 50). Notice how stone on the front elevation matches the stone on the side addition. The stone wall continues beyond the end of the house into the backyard as a creative solution to provide privacy.

GETTING IN THE DETAILS

Often the true trick of integrating the new addition with the old house is matching the details.

The fascia — the trim just under the eave line that edges the border between house and roof — should be continuous in style and shape between the existing house and the new addition.

If your existing house has brackets, you should use brackets in similar places on the new addition; or alternatively, you can use brackets on the addition and add them to the same areas on the existing house. The same is true of shutters, window boxes and other trim details.

Match lintels over windows and doors. Or add lintels to the existing house that match the new addition.

You can also use entries, porches, patios, trellises and landscaping to unify all of the elements of a house.

DON'T FEAR TO TREAD

The plans shown in this book — coupled with our exclusive Home Remodeler Service — are unique. Together they make it easy for you to plan and visualize your remodeling project. What's more, they make it much more convenient for you to talk to building officials, lenders and builder/remodelers. By ordering our practical and detailed plans, you will have the tools you need to speak the language of building and tailor your home to the way you really want to live.

DECK PLANS

Add The Finishing Touch With These Six Exciting Deck Designs!

SPLIT-LEVEL SUN DECK

Simple in design yet versatile in function, this two-level deck provides a striking addition to a backyard landscape where space is at a premium. Covering a total of 540 square feet, the deck can be accessed from indoors at both levels. The upper level can be reached through sliding doors at the breakfast room, making it handy to take meals outdoors. Just outside the breakfast room is plenty of space for table and chairs. A railing wraps around the tri-angled design, providing safety and interest.

One step down takes you to the second level. This level is accessed from indoors via the family room. A built-in bench just outside the sliding doors provides a place for seating and relaxation. The two-step, tiered design provides access to the ground level along its length.

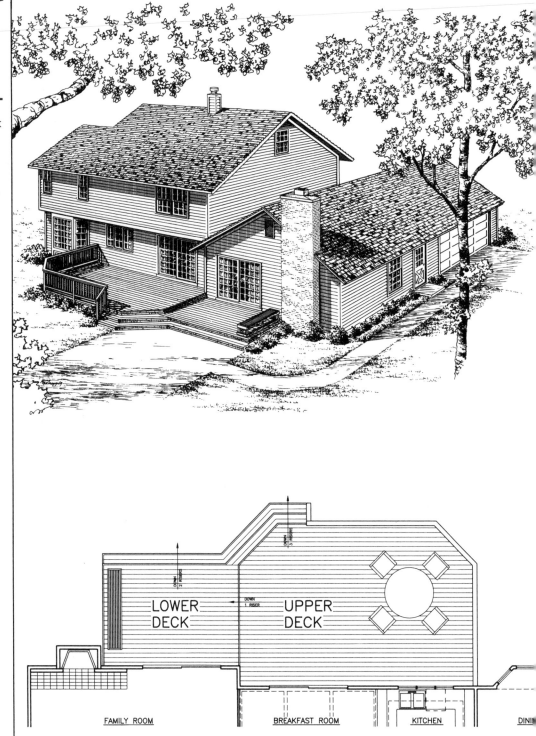

LOWER DECK

UPPER DECK

FAMILY ROOM

BREAKFAST ROOM

KITCHEN

DINI

Features at a Glance:

- Two Levels
- Built-In Bench Seating
- Easy to Build

To order construction drawings for this Deck Plan, see page 110.

HOME PLANNERS, INC.
1996 Blueprint Price Sheet

The following blueprint and sepia prices are guaranteed until December 31, 1996. Please disregard the prices shown in the accompanying book or books and use the new price schedule and postage and handling chart below when ordering by mail or phone.

Tier	1-set Study Package	4-set Building Package	8-set Building Package	1-set Reproducible Sepias	Home Customizer® Package
A	$280	$325	$385	$485	$535
B	320	365	425	545	595
C	360	405	465	605	655
D	400	445	505	665	715
E	520	565	625	725	775

Prices for 4- or 8-set Building Packages honored only at time of original order.

Additional identical blueprints in same order . . . .$50 per set
Reverse blueprints (mirror image) . . . .$50 per set
Specifications Outlines . . . .$10 each
Materials Lists (Available only for plans from those designers listed below.
    <u>Not</u> available for California Engineering Service.):
    Home Planners Designs $50
    Larry Belk Designs $50
    Larry Garnett Designs $50
    Design Basics Designs $75
    Alan Mascord Designs $50
    Donald Gardner Designs $50
    Design Traditions Designs $50
    If ordering a Materials List for a Schedule E plan, add $10 to above prices.
Exchanges . . . . . .$ 50 exchange fee for first set; $10 for each additional set
            $ 70 total exchange fee for 4 sets
            $100 total exchange fee for 8 sets

Postage and Handling	1-3 sets	4 or more sets
DELIVERY (Requires street address—no P.O. boxes)		
• Regular Service (allow 4-6 days delivery)	❏ 8.00	❏ 10.00
• 2nd Day Air (allow 2-3 days delivery)	❏ 12.00	❏ 20.00
• Next Day Air (allow 1 day delivery)	❏ 22.00	❏ 30.00
CERTIFIED MAIL (Requires signature) If no street address available. (Allow 4-6 days delivery)	❏ 10.00	❏ 14.00
OVERSEAS DELIVERY	fax, phone or mail for quote	

NOTE: *All delivery times are from date Blueprint Package is shipped.*

☎ **TOLL-FREE BLUEPRINT HOTLINE: 1-800-521-6797**

If we receive your order by 4:00 p.m. Eastern Time, Monday through Friday, we'll process it and ship within 48 hours. When ordering by phone, please have your charge card ready. We'll also ask you for the Order Form Key Number at the bottom of the coupon. Mail orders to:

HOME PLANNERS, INC.
3275 W. Ina Road, Suite 110
Tucson, Arizona 85741

Canadian Customers: Order Toll Free 1-800-561-4169! For faster service and plans that are modified for building in Canada, customers may now call in orders directly to our Canadian supplier of plans and charge the purchase to a charge card. Or add 40% to all prices and mail in Canadian funds to: The Plan Centre, 20 Cedar Street North, Kitchener, Ontario N2H 2W8

Builder's books emphasize how to do-it-yourself

-THE DETROIT NEWS-

"You can have a good nuts and bolts builder but a bad businessman," Hasenau says in his book, "Building Consultant" "Unfortunately, even though a builder is licensed does not insure that he is completely scrupulous," he says. **JACK WOERPEL**

BUILDING CONSULTANT

Housing in Print · **The Washington Post**

Contracting For Yourself

THE FUNDEMENTALS ARE THERE
—MIAMI HERALD—

Book Gives Warning — St. Pete Times

By John H. Kuhnle

Supervise the building of your own home and save thousands of dollars?

Or personally direct the construction of your worst nightmare that gobbles up several times your original budget?

Either one can happen to a first-time homebuilder, according to a professional builder-turned author, James J. Hasenau in "Build Your Own Home: A Guide for Subcontracting the Easy Way."

. . A reassuring guide of what to request or expect from subcontractors. Diagrams and sample forms – Library Association

POPULAR MECHANICS

Defray the costs of building and remodeling

Build your own home

page guide for the builder interested in doing his own subcontracting. Land acquisition, financing, plans, building, hiring. Every aspect of building for yourself.

DETROIT FREE PRESS

Builder Revises His How-to Book

A couple of years ago, a Detroit-area second generation builder by the name of J. James Hasenau wrote a "how-to" book, entitled "Build Your Own Home." The subtitle explained that the book actually told how to go about subcontracting the actual construction.

Hasenau felt at the time that he had been thorough about his subject matter, and that the book should endure over a period of time.

Then came inflation. Building materials went up. Interest rates on construction financing went up. Construction codes started changing like crazy. And, finally, the costs of on-site thefts of building supplies became something to reckon with.

So Hasenau has re-written his book, and

. . . Supervise the building of your house and save thousands of dollars . . . or bargain for undreamed of miseries and voracious cost overruns? – The Denver Post

GARDEN WAY PUBLISHING
by J. James Hasenau

#199. Subcontracting out most of the work on a building project, but acting as your own prime contractor can save you a substantial amount of money. Learn here the ins and outs of subcontracting, the work you can expect done, the scheduling of different subcontractors to keep a project moving smoothly, where one sub leaves off and another starts. Also all about ordering materials, paying procedures and discounts, financing, zoning, setting grades, building risk factors and much more. A very realistic way to have your home built if you have limited time and money to invest.

REAL ESTATE INVESTORS REPORT

and the cost of rectifying the situation.

Reference: An excellent introduction to the art of contracting is *Build Your Own Home: A Guide For Subcontracting the Easy Way* by J. James Hasenau,

Unlike general books on housing construction — books which don't go into the details of surveys, sewer lines, foundations, building permits, etc. — Hasenau describes in detail the various steps a builder has to follow — usually in a prescribed order — to complete the house without too many hassles. — *Milwaukee Sentinel*

HOUSE BEAUTIFUL HOME MODELING FALL/WINTER

defray costs of building or remodeling

BUILD YOUR OWN HOME

WORKBENCH

Not a book about how to hammer a nail, or build a stud wall, this book is authored by a man with 30 years of experience in home and apartment building. He describes how you can be a contractor for building your home, or just how to tell what is right and wrong about a home being constructed. We recommend it for anyone considering having a home built, or who will build his own. Tips on financing, how to buy a lot, zoning, building codes,.etc.

Miami Herald

Building a Home Not an Easy Task

. . . .or addition. It shows the short cuts and the ways to accomplish them. It also shows what to look for in advantages and disadvantages of some systems used in construction.

the fundamentals are there.

ELI ADAMS

44. Build Your Own Home. A guide for subcontracting the easy way, tells you how to organize your own building program, from land acquisition, through financing, plans, building, hiring . . . every aspect of home building covered.

Builder's books preach what he has practiced

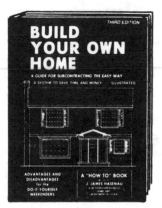

BI-LEVEL DECK WITH COVERED DINING

This deck is designed for an active family, as well as for entertaining. With two levels and two accesses from indoors, each area becomes a versatile extension of its adjacent room. The total deck area adds 945 square feet of outdoor living space.

Located at the rear of this two-story, Georgian-style home, the deck's two levels extend into the back yard. Stairway exits from level one and level two allow easy access to the ground, from both the break-fast room and gathering room. Both rooms open onto the deck for open-air enjoyment of meals, entertaining, and quiet times of relaxation. Because the gathering room is three steps down from sur-rounding rooms, the exit to the lower deck is made without stepping down. An overhead trellis or covered area provides a feeling of privacy and shade, making the deck's sitting area comfortable even during warm periods of the year. Built-in benches provide ample seating for guests.

Features at a Glance:

- Latticework Railing
- Covered Dining Area
- Two Built-In Benches

To order construction drawings for this Deck Plan, see page 110.

BACKYARD EXTENDER DECK

This deck, though not large, allows for an array of uses. Its geometric shape adds interest in a relatively small space—654 square feet. It also permits traffic to flow to and from the kitchen—one of the most popular patterns of deck owners. It is so convenient to go from kitchen to deck-side table with a meal or snack. The plan provides for a table and chairs to be tucked into the corner just outside the breakfast room entrance. A short wall (or optional handrail) here maintains privacy and protection.

Continuous-level steps around the perimeter allow for complete access to the ground level. This kind of tiered-step design can be modified—extending the steps so the deck has several levels. Here, the two levels function as steps, and can also double as seating for casual parties. Convenient access from the covered rear porch on two sides means added enjoyment of the deck from that area.

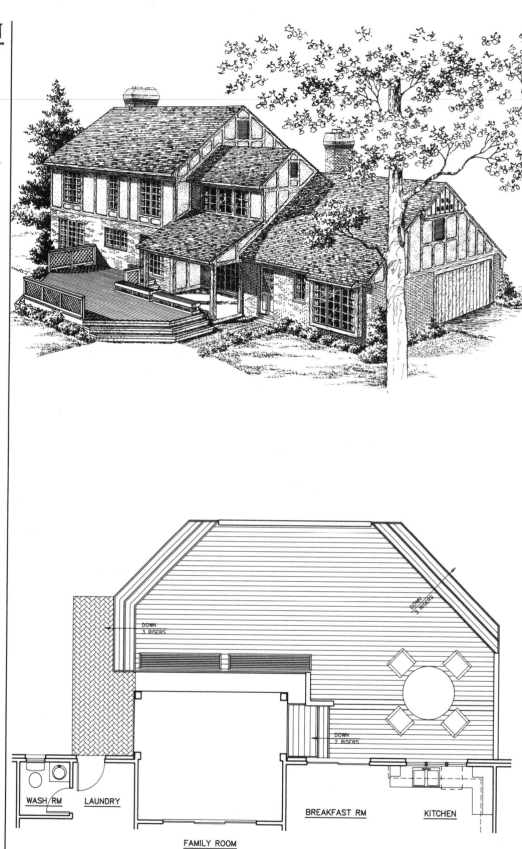

Features at a Glance:

• Completely Open To Backyard
• Double Benches Along Covered Porch
• Appealing Angular Design

To order construction drawings for this Deck Plan, see page 110.

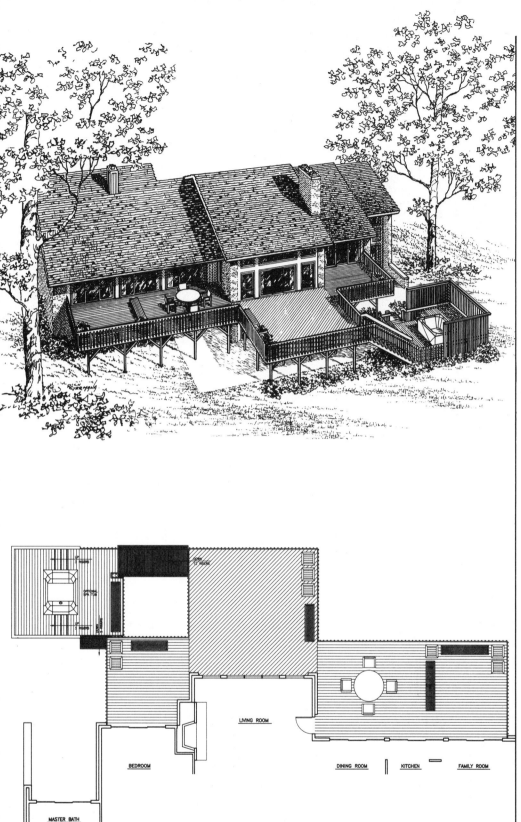

SPECTACULAR "RESORT-STYLE" DECK

What a spectacular deck—sure to elicit admiring oohs and aaahs from all who see it! Designed to be absolutely spacious, with over 1,400 square feet, this deck features two levels—one at upper level and the other near ground level.

Second story—This level is actually three connected decks, and can be reached by several rooms—all with sliding doors. Deck surface patterns change from area to area, reinforcing the feeling of multiple outdoor rooms. One rectangular deck is adjacent to the family room, kitchen and dining room. Built-in benches and planters are functional finishing touches.

Just off the living room is a square-shaped section of deck connected to the family-wing deck. It, too, has a built-in bench and planters. The stairway leading to the ground-level deck makes its connection here.

Ground level—Taking the stairway down leads to the more private ground-level deck. Tall vertical boards provide screening and promote a sense of enclosure. A built-in bench provides the perfect place to relax, or to dry off after a refreshing soak in the spa. A short stairway (two steps) from this deck provides access to the ground.

Note: This deck is attached to its adjoining house with a ledger strip to make the addition more structurally sound.

Features at a Glance:

- Secluded Hot-Tub Area
- Private Areas For Eating And Relaxing
- Complete Backyard Entertainment Center

To order construction drawings for this Deck Plan, see page 110.

OUTDOOR LIFESTYLE DECK

This rectangular-shaped deck is long and spacious (over 800 square feet)—perfect for entertaining. In this instance, it adjoins a covered porch, a real advantage in certain regions when the weather does not cooperate.

Multiple access—from the master bedroom, gathering room and dining room—helps ensure this deck's utility. A table-and-chairs setting is positioned near the dining room to make it convenient to serve outdoor meals.

The stairway is built wide in a striking "V" design. Additional custom features include built-in benches and planters. Railings, too, surround the perimeter of the decking for safety. In this example, lattice-work has been added to the railing for the enhanced feeling of privacy and enclosure.

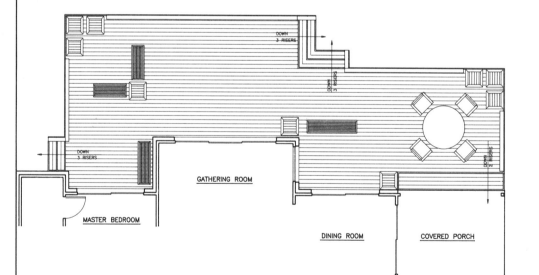

DOWN 3 RISERS

DOWN 3 RISERS

DOWN 3 RISERS

DOWN 3 RISERS

DOWN 2 RISERS

GATHERING ROOM

MASTER BEDROOM

DINING ROOM

COVERED PORCH

Features at a Glance:

- Long, Rectangular Plan
- Four-Point Access To Interior
- Cozy Corner Seating

To order construction drawings for this Deck Plan, see page 110.

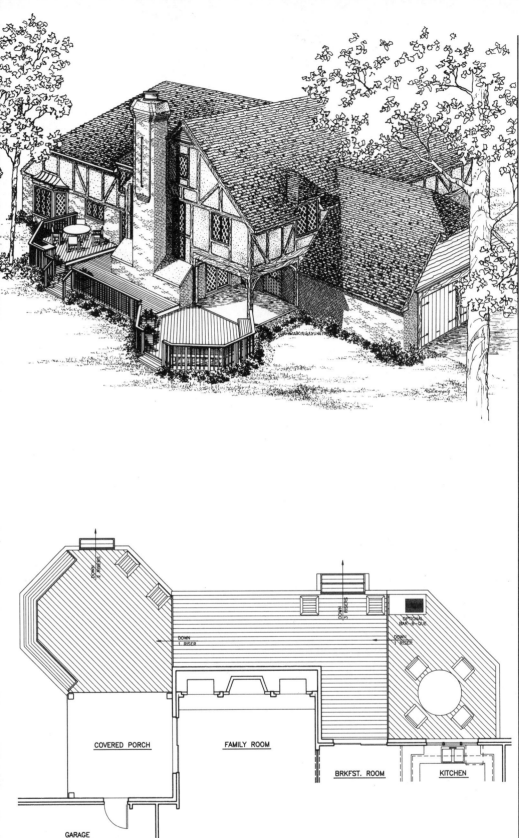

DECK PLAN

TRI-LEVEL DECK WITH GRILL

This deck offers the best of both worlds. With three levels totaling over 650 square feet and an elongated shape, it is well-suited for simultaneous activities without disturbing the participating parties. Because the deck areas are linked and easy to reach, it is also excellent for large gatherings. Stairways are not required to go from one level to the next: The deck is thoughtfully designed so that each level has a change in elevation equal to a step. The result is a deck composed of three separate areas, made even more distinctive by contrasting surface patterns for each area. In fact, each section could be built separately, beginning with the upper section.

Looking for convenience? A few steps out the kitchen door there's room for table and chairs—a relaxing place for fresh-air meals. Looking for versatility? The octagonal deck design effectively extends the livability of the covered porch, which can be reached from the family room. What's more, with garage access next to the covered porch, transportation of furniture to and from the deck is made simple.

In addition to the expansive bench seating, a moveable grill is installed near the kitchen door for barbecues. The grill can also be built as a wet bar. Planters add a finishing touch. Access to the ground level is via two exits: one near the kitchen, the other outside the covered porch.

Features at a Glance:

- Three Lovely Levels
- Outdoor Barbecue Grill
- Quaint Conversation Area

To order construction drawings for this Deck Plan, see page 110.

THE REMODELING BLUEPRINT PACKAGE

Remodeled Plan Frontal Sheet.

An artist's line drawing shows the remodeled house. This drawing provides a visual image of what your new addition will look like when completed and its relationship to the existing house.

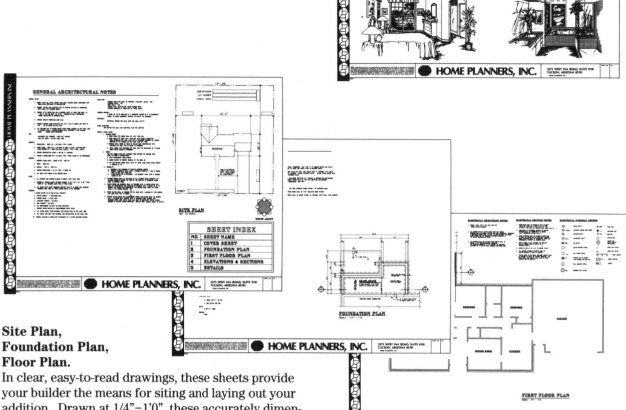

Site Plan, Foundation Plan, Floor Plan.

In clear, easy-to-read drawings, these sheets provide your builder the means for siting and laying out your addition. Drawn at 1/4"=1'0", these accurately dimensioned plans locate all permanent walls, fixtures, electrical switches and outlets, as well as call out notes for floor, ceiling and roof construction.

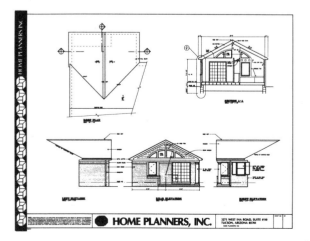

Elevations and Cross-sections.

Fully noted and rendered elevations of all sides of the addition accurately illustrate the finished project. The cross-section clearly depicts, in cut-away fashion, how the various parts of the addition fit together. Drawn at 1/4"=1'0" these elevations and sections can easily be cross-referenced to the floor plans.

Details.

Large-scale format details further emphasize the construction techniques, making it easy for your builder to complete the job. Drawn at 1"=1'0", all materials are clearly indicated and noted.

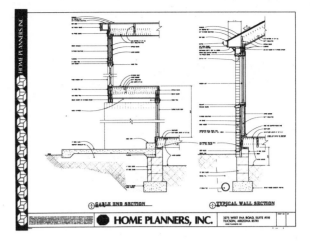

Material List.

This is a complete shopping list of all the materials, including sizes and amounts needed to build your addition. Your builder can easily reference the Material List to the plans.

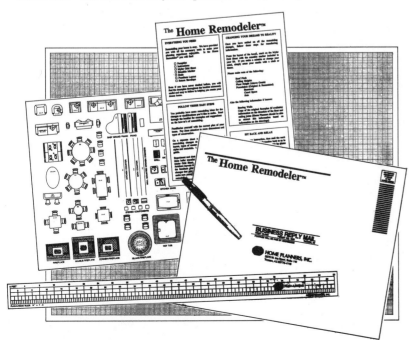

THE HOME REMODELER™ KIT

If you've chosen one of our exciting Remodeling Plans, but the design doesn't fit your home precisely, you may be asking: Can I modify the plan? Do I have to make the changes myself or hire an expensive architect? What if my home requires some special attention?

Don't fret—the answers to your questions are just a phone call away. The Home Remodeler™ Service, a new service from our Home Customizer® Division, will assist you in carrying out a successful remodeling experience. Just call our toll-free number 1-800-322-6797, ext. 134 and ask that the Home Remodeler™ Kit be sent with your set of plans. The low $5.95 price of this kit will be refunded with your custom remodeling order. You'll find included in your kit:

- Easy Instructions
- Sample Modifications
- Mylar Work Sheet
- Erasable Marker
- Scale
- Furniture Cutouts
- Prepaid Postage-Return Envelope

Just follow the easy instructions, then mail the work sheet and other requested information back to us in the postage-paid envelope. We will reply by phone with a cost quotation for modifying your plans. Because it's that simple, there's no reason not to take advantage of our easy, low-cost remodeling. After all, who knows our plans better than we do? By using our exclusive Home Remodeler™ Service, you and your family will be enjoying your newly remodeled home in no time!

The Home Remodeler™ Kit
Just $5.95 Complete
(Price refunded with custom remodeling order)

THE DECK BLUEPRINT PACKAGE

Our plans and details are carefully prepared in an easy-to-understand format that will guide you through every stage of your deck-building project. The Deck Blueprint Package contains four sheets outlining information pertinent to the specific Deck Plan you have chosen. A separate package—Deck Construction Details—provides the how-to data for building any deck, including instructions for adaptations and conversions. Our Complete Deck Building Package contains 1 set of Custom Deck Plans of your choice, plus 1 set of Standard Deck Building Details for one low price. See pages 110-111 for price schedule and ordering information.

Standard Details for Building Your Deck

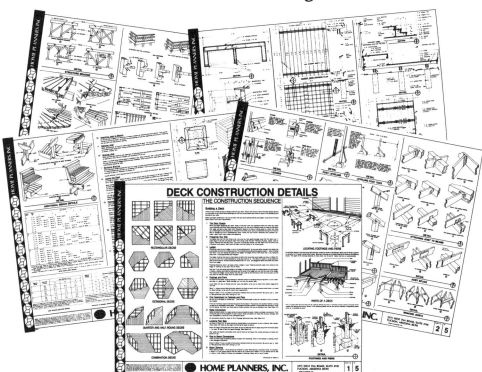

In five information-packed sheets, these standard details provide all the general data necessary for building, adapting, and converting any deck. Included are layout examples, framing patterns, and foundation variations; details for ledgers, columns, and beams; schedules and charts; handrail, stair, and ramp details; and special options such as spa platforms, planters, bars, benches and overhead trellises. This is a must-have package for the first-time deck builder and a useful addition to the custom deck plans shown on the next page. Only $14.95.

Custom Deck Plans

Each deck plan shown on pages 100 to 105 has been custom designed by a professional architect. With each Custom Deck Plan, you receive the following:

Deck Plan Frontal Sheet. An artist's line drawing shows the deck as it connects to its matching or corresponding house. This drawing provides a visual image of what the deck will look like when completed, highlighting the livability factors.

Deck Framing and Floor Plans. In clear, easy-to-read drawings, this sheet shows all component parts of the deck from an aerial viewpoint with dimensions, notes, and references. Drawn at 1/4" = 1' - 0", the floor plan provides a finished overhead view of the deck including rails, stairs, benches, and ramps. The framing plan gives complete details on how the deck is to be built, including the position and spacing of footings, joists, beams, posts, and decking materials. Where necessary, the sheet also includes sections and closeups to further explain structural details.

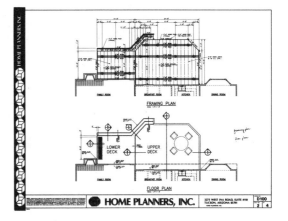

Deck Elevations. Large-scale front and side elevations of the deck complete the visual picture of the deck. Drawn at 3/8" = 1' - 0", the elevations show the height of rails, balusters, stair risers, benches and other deck accessories.

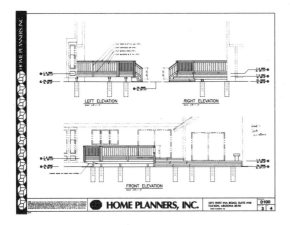

Deck Materials List. This is a complete shopping list of all the materials needed (including sizes and amounts) to build your deck. The Materials List is complemented by section drawings showing placement of hardware such as thru-bolts, screws, nuts, washers, and nails and how these items are used to secure deck flooring, rails, posts, and joists. Scale is 3/4" = 1' - 0".

MATERIAL LIST		
QUANTITY	SIZE	DESCRIPTION
23	4"x4"-4'	TREATED LUMBER
12	4"X4"-5'	TREATED LUMBER
52 L.F.	2"x2"	TREATED BALUSTERS 30" LG.
300 L.F.	2"x4"	TREATED LUMBER
1850 L.F.	2"x6"	TREATED LUMBER
600 L.F.	2"x8"	TREATED LUMBER
10 L.F.	2"x10"	TREATED LUMBER
8 L.F.	2"x12"	TREATED LUMBER
70 L.F.		LANDSCAPE EDGE
550 S.F.		FILTER FABRIC
550 S.F.		2" DEEP PEA GRAVEL
60	3/8"ø x8" LG.	THRU-BOLTS W/ NUTS & WASHERS
30	3/8"ø x6" LG.	THRU-BOLTS W/ NUTS & WASHERS
4	1 1/2"x1 1/2"x1/8"-7" LG.	STEEL ANGLES
16	3/16"ø x2"	LAG SCREWS
2 LBS.	8d	FOR RAILINGS
5 LBS.	16d	FOR POSTS & JOISTS
25 LBS.	10d	FOR DECKING
		NOTE: ALL NAILS TO BE HOT DIPPED GALVANIZED SCREW NAILS
		•QUANTITY OF NAILS MAY VARY DEPENDING ON TYPE OF CONNECTIONS USED.

TO ORDER, CALL TOLL FREE 1-800-521-6797, OR SEE PAGES 110-111.

PRICE SCHEDULE & PLANS INDEX

Remodeling Plans Price Schedule

Price Group	L	M	N	P
1 set	$65	$75	$85	$95
3 sets	$85	$95	$105	$115
6 sets	$105	$115	$125	$135

Additional identical sets ....$15 each
Reverse sets (mirror image) ....$15 each

Deck Plans Price Schedule

CUSTOM DECK PLANS

Price Group	Q	R	S
1 Set Custom Plans	$15	$20	$25

Additional identical sets ....$5.00 each
Reverse sets (mirror image)...$5.00 each

STANDARD DECK DETAILS
1 Set Generic Construction Details $14.95 each

COMPLETE DECK BUILDING PACKAGE

Price Group	Q	R	S
1 Set Custom Plans, plus			
1 Set Standard Deck Details	$25	$30	$35

How To Use The Index

To use the Index below, refer to the design number listed in numerical order (a helpful page reference is also given). Note the price index letter and refer to the Blueprint Price Schedule above for the cost of one, three or six sets of Remodeling Blueprints or one set of Deck Blueprints. Prices are also shown for additional identical and reverse blueprint sets.

To Order: Fill in and send the order form on page 111—or Call Toll Free 1-800-521-6797.

REMODELING PLANS PRICE INDEX

Plan No.	Page No.	Price Code
R100	28	P
R101	30	N
R102	32	P
R103	34	P
R104	36	N
R105	38	L
R106	52	P
R107	54	N
R108	56	N
R109	58	P
R110	60	N
R111	62	P
R112	40	N
R113	42	P
R114	44	P
R115	46	P

Plan No.	Page No.	Price Code
R116	48	P
R117	50	P
R118	64	M
R119	66	P
R120	68	M
R121	70	P
R122	82	L
R123	84	L
R124	86	L
R125	88	L
R126	74	M
R127	72	M
R128	76	N
R129	78	N
R130	80	N

DECK PLANS PRICE INDEX

Plan No.	Page No.	Price Code
D100	100	Q
D102	101	R
D103	102	Q
D109	103	S
D118	104	R
D119	105	S

**Canadian Customers
Order Toll-Free 1-800-848-2550**
For faster, more economical service, Canadian customers may now call in orders on our Toll-Free line. Or, complete the order form at right, and mail with your check indicating U.S. funds to:

Home Planners, Inc.
3275 W. Ina Road, Suite 110
Tucson, AZ 85741

By FAX: Copy the Order Form on the next page and send it on our International FAX line: 1-602-297-6219.

Toll Free 1-800-521-6797

Normal Office Hours:
8:00 a.m. to 8:00 p.m. Eastern Time
Monday through Friday
Our staff will gladly answer any questions during normal office hours. Our answering service can accept orders after hours or on weekends.

If we receive your order by 5:00 p.m. Eastern Time, Monday through Friday, we'll process it the same day and ship it the following business day. When ordering by phone, please have your charge card ready. We'll also ask you for the Order Form Key Number at the bottom of the coupon. Please use our Toll-Free number for blueprint and book orders only.
For Customization orders call 1-800-322-6797, ext. 134.

By FAX: Copy the Order Form on the next page and send it on our International FAX line: 1-602-297-6219.

Before You Order . . .

Before completing the coupon at right or calling us on our toll-free Blueprint Hotline, you may be interested to learn more about our services and products. Here's some information you will find helpful.

Quick turnaround
We process and ship every blueprint order from our office within 48 hours. On most orders, we do even better. Normally, if we receive your order by 5 p.m. Eastern time, we'll process it the same day and ship it the following day. Because of this quick turnaround, we won't send a formal notice acknowledging receipt of your order.

Our exchange policy
Since blueprints are printed in response to your order, we cannot honor requests for refunds. However, we will exchange your entire first order for an equal number of blueprints at a price of $20 for the first set and $5 for each additional set for Remodeling Plans and $10 for the first set and $3 for each additional set for Deck Plans...*plus* the difference in cost if exchanging for a design in a higher price bracket or *less* the difference in cost if exchanging for a design in a lower price bracket. All sets from the first order must be returned before the exchange can take place. Please add $6 for postage and handling via ground service; $12 via 2nd Day Air.

About reverse blueprints (mirror image)
If you want to build in reverse of the plan as shown, we will include an extra set of reversed blueprints (mirror image) for an additional fee of $15 for Remodeling Plans and $5 for Deck Plans. Although lettering and dimensions appear backward, reverses will be a useful visual aid if you decide to flop the plan.

Modifying or customizing our plans
With such a great selection of Remodeling Plans, you are bound to find the one that suits you. However, alterations can be made to any of the plans—call our Remodeler Specialist at 800/322-6797, ext. 134 to discuss your specific needs and order our exclusive Home Remodeler™ Kit. Or purchase the kit right now by using the order form at right.

Architectural and engineering seals
Some cities and states are now requiring that a licensed architect or engineer review and "seal" your blueprints prior to construction. This is often due to local or regional concerns over energy consumption, safety codes, seismic ratings, etc. For this reason, you may find it necessary to consult with a local professional to have your plans reviewed. This can normally be accomplished with minimum delays and for a nominal fee.

Compliance with local codes and regulations
At the time of creation, our plans are drawn to specifications published by Building Officials Code Administrators (BOCA), the Southern Standard Building Code, or the Uniform Building Code, and are designed to meet or exceed national building standards.

Some states, counties, and municipalities have their own codes, zoning requirements, and building regulations. Before starting construction, consult with local building authorities and make sure you comply with local ordinances and codes, including obtaining any necessary permits or inspections as building progresses. In some cases, minor modifications to your plans by your builder, local architect, or designer may be required to meet local conditions and requirements. We are able to make these changes to remodeling plans providing you supply all pertinent information from your local building authorities.

How many blueprints do you need?
A single set of blueprints is sufficient to study a plan in greater detail. However, if you are planning to obtain cost estimates from a contractor or subcontractors—or if you are planning to build immediately—you will need more sets. Because additional sets are cheaper when ordered in quantity with the original order, make sure you order enough blueprints to satisfy all requirements. The following checklist will help you determine how many you need:

____ Owner

____ Builder (generally requires at least three sets; one as a legal document, one to use during inspections, and at least one to give to subcontractors)

____ Local Building Department

____ Mortgage Lender

____ TOTAL NUMBER OF SETS

Index